Rethinking Gendered Regulations and Resistances in Education

Rethinking Gendered Regulations and Resistances in Education highlights key debates on the theme of 'regulation and resistance', focusing on some of the most pressing contemporary issues in the field of gender and education today. It underlines the need for educational research to attend to historical and psychosocial specificity, chart local complexity and global disparity, de-colonise our Euro-western-centered gender analysis, and consistently engage with the economic and policy domains of education as researchers and practitioners, if we are to effectively tackle the diversity and complexity of gender equality issues in education.

Chapters in this collection showcase some of the varied and wide-ranging theoretical approaches at play in current gender and education scholarship, and raise questions about the types of research methods that can open up new ways of documenting processes of social and subjective struggle and transformation in education. It stimulates important thinking about what has been, what is and what can be, as we face the future of gender and educational engagement, struggle and debate.

This book was originally published as a special issue of *Gender and Education*.

Jessica Ringrose is Senior Lecturer in Sociology of Gender and Education at the Institute of Education, University of London, UK. She is author of *Postfeminist Education?: Girls and the Sexual Politics of Schooling* (2012) and editor of *Deleuze and Research Methodologies* (2012, with Rebecca Coleman).

Rethinking Gendered Regulations and Resistances in Education

Edited by
Jessica Ringrose

LONDON AND NEW YORK

First published 2012
by Routledge

2 Park Square, Milton Park, Abingdon, Oxfordshire OX14 4RN
711 Third Avenue, New York, NY 10017

Routledge is an imprint of the Taylor & Francis Group, an informa business

First issued in paperback 2018

Copyright © 2012 Taylor & Francis

This book is a reproduction of *Gender and Education*, volume 22, issue 6. The Publisher requests to those authors who may be citing this book to state, also, the bibliographical details of the special issue on which the book was based.

All rights reserved. No part of this book may be reprinted or reproduced or utilised in any form or by any electronic, mechanical, or other means, now known or hereafter invented, including photocopying and recording, or in any information storage or retrieval system, without permission in writing from the publishers.

Notice:
Product or corporate names may be trademarks or registered trademarks, and are used only for identification and explanation without intent to infringe.

British Library Cataloguing in Publication Data
A catalogue record for this book is available from the British Library

ISBN 13: 978-0-415-69348-6 (hbk)
ISBN 13: 978-1-138-37726-4 (pbk)

Typeset in Times New Roman
by Taylor & Francis Books

Disclaimer
The publisher would like to make readers aware that the chapters in this book are referred to as articles as they had been in the special issue. The publisher accepts responsibility for any inconsistencies that may have arisen in the course of preparing this volume for print.

Contents

1. Introduction
   Jessica Ringrose   1

2. Kartini's children: on the need for thinking gender and education together on a world scale
   Raewyn Connell   9

3. Resisting dominant discourses: implications of indigenous, African feminist theory and methods for gender and education research
   Bagele Chilisa and Gabo Ntseane   23

4. On the madness of lecturing on gender: a psychoanalytic discussion
   Deborah P. Britzman   39

5. Intersectionality, Black British feminism and resistance in education: a roundtable discussion
   Suki Ali, Heidi Mirza, Ann Phoenix and Jessica Ringrose (Chair)   53

6. Everyday banality in a documentary by teenage women: between the trivial and the extreme. Schooling and desiring in contexts of extreme urban poverty
   Silvia Grinberg   69

7. Charting cartographies of resistance: lines of flight in women artists' narratives
   Maria Tamboukou   85

Index   103

INTRODUCTION

This special issue is the culmination of the 7th Gender and Education Association (GEA) Conference held 25–27 March 2009 at the Institute of Education (IOE), University of London. The theme of the conference, 'Regulation and Resistance', emerged out of a symposium during the previous 2007 GEA Conference in Dublin, 'Butler and Beyond: Using Poststructural Theory in Gender and Education Research', organised by Emma Renold and Jessica Ringrose. During the 2007 sessions 12 UK and international educational scholars debated issues of poststructural feminism, subjectivity, queer theory, materiality, discourse, and the implications, possibilities and limitations of using Judith Butler's work for thinking about gender and educational research.

When the IOE conference team[1] decided in summer of 2007 to apply to host the 2009 conference, we were keen to follow through with a poststructurally inspired theme. We felt 'Regulation and Resistance' articulated an awareness of social and subjective power dynamics that we saw as principal contributions of poststructural thinking, including Butler's theories, which draw on and extend Freud, Althusser and Foucault. Foucault's (1978/1990) theories of regulation and governance foreground a sort of immanent or always present 'resistance' within power relations and attempt to move outside the conscious/unconscious binary and a humanist focus on 'the subject' to articulate social relations of force in a depersonalised way that underpins what he calls 'bio-politics'. Butler's work (1993, 1997) explores the regulatory force of the 'heterosexual matrix' through which gender subjectification and identification manifests, but also returns our attention to the 'psychic life of power', foregrounding psychoanalytic understandings of 'internal' psychic resistance (to, for instance, regulatory forces, but also to 'progressive' change), with important implications for education. We felt, therefore, that the complex, often contested notions of 'regulation' and 'resistance' gestured toward both a long tradition of critical and feminist theory and activism and exciting recent directions in educational thinking on gender.

Hence, our call for papers asked the questions:

- How do education and gender regulate?
- How do we theorise, research, talk about and enact resistances to regulatory practices and gendered power relations in education?

We hoped the theme would ignite a range of lively responses and fruitful engagements with gender, feminism and power at every level of educational practice, including politics, theorising, policy creation, research methodologies, pedagogical engagement and grass-roots activism. Our call also stressed the need to address the neo-liberal, marketised and standardised (regulated) contexts of contemporary educational environments, as well as growing global disparities. We encouraged participants to explore educational politics, power, struggle, agency and subjectivity (resistance); and suggested important approaches might be psychosocial and intersectional (paying attention to race, class, sexuality, disability etc.). We also felt it was crucial to try to 'globalise' the debates at the conference as much as possible, to bridge what can sometime be seen as north–south divides in theory and scholarship, and the dominance of the 'over-developed' world in shaping both scholarship and policy agendas on gender and education (Fennell and Arnot 2009; see also Connell in this issue). We wanted to facilitate the involvement of a range of speakers from diverse international zones, and particularly 'developing' contexts to create as we put it: 'dialogue about gender and education that spans disciplinary, theoretical, political and national boundaries'.

The response to the call for papers was unprecedented, with the conference becoming the largest GEA conference to date, hosting 298 delegates from 19 nations. We were able to encourage international participation through a bursary programme supported by the GEA and the IOE. We were also fortunate to secure an exceptional range of international and local speakers whose work spoke to the theme in important ways. These included two keynote speakers: Raewyn Connell whose talk looked at global power inequities and raised questions about developing an educational gender analysis at a 'global scale', and Deborah Britzman whose paper explored classical psychoanalytic theories of power and resistance to explore the 'madness' of lecturing on gender. We also had a plenary roundtable discussion between Suki Ali, Heidi Mirza and Ann Phoenix, who explored educational regulation and resistance through Black British feminism and intersectional approaches; and a plenary panel, Bagele Chilisa, Silvia Grinberg and Grace Livingstone who debated issues of centre and margin and feminist, educational activism in diverse international zones.

Unfortunately, it was both troubling and instructive that the issues of regulation and resistance thematically underpinning the conference were brought into dramatic relief before the conference even began when the plenary panellist Grace Livingstone, Associate Professor of African American Studies at University of Puget Sound in Seattle, was detained at Heathrow airport for 11 hours the Saturday before the conference. Unable to reach the organisers at the weekend, and despite traveling legally with a US Green Card, passport control queried Grace's invitation to speak at a university event, and eventually refused her entry ordering her on a plane back to Seattle. Shocked and distressed, the organisers worked with Grace and her university, making every effort to have her return to London in time for the panel. However, unable to sort out immigration in the short timeframe we resorted to a teleconference, where Grace delivered a powerful talk on racial marginalisation. These events were a visceral reminder of the need for collective resistance to what Foucault called the 'dividing practices' that organise not only the contemporary profiling practices of international immigration policy, but educational experiences as well.

We hope that the special issue will serve as a form of resistant political practice that 'talks back' to these persistent bio-politics of regulation and control. We are fortunate enough to have most of the speakers represented in the special issue.[2] Contributions address gender and power dynamics from a range of diverse perspectives, some not envisioned in our original call, perhaps a strong indicator that the theme did the very work of conceptual provocation and proliferation we had hoped it would. In thinking about the diverse contributions, 'regulations' and 'resistances' have been consciously pluralised to recognise the multiplicity in approaches, while the verb 're-thinking' is a gesture to how the pieces set our thinking about gender and education into renewed motion.

The articles

Raewyn Connell's paper, 'Kartini's children: on the need for thinking gender and education together on a world scale', begins the special issue. Connell, Professor of Education, University of Sydney, Australia, is an internationally renowned scholar of gender and sexuality. Having made groundbreaking contributions to studies of educational inequalities and gender regulations, particularly the field of masculinity studies, Connell's more recent work has explored the constitution and workings of gender across a diverse range of educational and wider social contexts and has also included interrogations of transgender. In her piece for the special issue Raewyn directly takes up the challenge of globalisation for the field of gender and education and the dominance of an 'intellectual framing in scholarship that is internal to the global North'. Connell's article raises some of the central tensions that organise work in gender in education that the conference theme attempted to address, asking, in the 'swelling scene of gender transformations, how do we theorise gender?' She suggests as important as 'deconstructionist' gender theory has been for understanding 'resistance to normativity', 'valorising gender diversity' and enabling a 'kind of radical tolerance or inclusiveness which is an important renovating force for feminism'; it is also limited. Connell contends, with a deconstructionist 'conception of power and of radical action it is difficult to generate the idea of a policy process that involves collective action and institution-building'. She calls for 'decolonising' approaches and methodologies that can help us to understand the global and local complexities of gender and education in contexts of neoliberalism, the economic reign of transnational corporations and deeply gendered, patriarchal nation states.

In the end, however, Connell's own piece enlivens both structural and poststructural logics as she mobilises her own groundbreaking theories of multiple masculinities and femininities to argue there is no 'fixed gender hierarchy, rival patriarchies may lay claim to power, and new strategies of resistance may emerge'. She also suggests that we must bring the implications of micro and ethnographic educational study for policy to the foreground, insisting: 'I think it is very important that gender researchers should stay in the arena of policy'. In a crucial critique of how normative policy formations end up making the statistical gender gap stand in or come to '*become* the meaning of gender', thereby erasing the multiplicity and complexity of gender issues in education, Connell insists we shift the focus to explorations of 'gender, education citizenship and justice on a world scale'.

The second paper 'Resisting dominant discourses: implications of indigenous, african feminist theory and methods for gender and education research ' by Bagele Chilisa, Associate Professor, Department of Educational Foundations, University of Botswana, and Gabo Ntseane, Associate Professor, Department of Adult Education, University of Botswana, takes up Connell's call for decolonising theory, policy and research in education. Drawing on and extending the important challenges to Euro-Western feminism made nearly 20 years ago by Chandra Talpade Mohanty, Chilisa and Ntseane's article confronts 'the tensions between Western gender theory and research and postcolonial and indigenous feminist standpoints'. Importantly the paper also foregrounds and critiques the patriarchal context through rich empirical research accounts that illustrate tensions in Botswana masculine culture in how 'boys and teachers invoke both local culture and Western religion to justify the gender order in … school'. The paper suggests the need for an approach that can work both with and against hybrid indigenous/Western patriarchal ideologies. Chilisa and Ntseane also call for a redefinition feminist methodologies and ethics via three central questions:

(1) What is my purpose as a researcher?
(2) Do I challenge and resist dominant discourses that marginalise those who suffer oppression?
(3) What needs to be done to bring about social transformation and heal those who are suffering?

Research examples where these questions become fundamental to orienting research praxis are outlined as part of developing a new methodology as 'feminist-activist educators' based on 'healing' and 'transformative' ethics.

The third paper is from Deborah Britzman, Distinguished Research Professor, York University, Canada, and pre-eminent educational theorist whose work has brought psychoanalysis to bear on questions of learning. Britzman's psychoanalytic contribution is important for reminding us of, and returning us to, some of the psycho-social, internal complexities of dynamics of resistance in relation to the confounding experiences of being educated into genders. She argues in her piece, 'On the madness of lecturing on gender: a psychoanalytic discussion', that we need to consistently unseat the familiar gender polarities, the 'phantasies of masculinity and femininity' that organise educational policies and practices on gender, suggesting 'a one-sided take on gender as either masculine or feminine as the entire experience and goal of the body forecloses attempts to understand the self's gender work as both internal conflict and intersubjectivity'. She suggests the 'madness' of lecturing on gender stems from the very paradox of negotiating the 'sides' of the fixed binary through which gender identity is constituted. She argues provocatively that 'if we feel we may only have or occupy one side, we find and create the condition of war', with 'war a terrible breakdown of knowledge and imagination'.

This insight seems particularly fruitful in the context of the sterile policy ground discussed in Connell's piece where the dualistic conception of gender and the gap between fixed male/female properties comes to signify the total meaning of what gender *is* for education, in ways that miss the entire psychosocial world of gender elaborated by Britzman. Drawing on some fascinating historical lectures by Melanie Klein, Joan Riviere, and Donald Winnicott, Britzman argues 'The psychic life of gender is an admixture of masculinity and femininity and so expresses the conflicts between them'. What a profound challenge this statement issues to those of us who wish to engage with and unseat the dominant policy domains of gender consistently 'done' through statistical rates and comparisons! As Britzman concludes, 'the psychic cost of reducing gender to the encasements of biology, stereotype, or even knowledge is depression and rigidity, which translates into a defended organisation dedicated to hatred toward the self and the other, a wearing away in the faith that language can matter, and a giving up on the creative work of playing with reality. This is also the condition of war'.

The fourth piece, 'Intersectionality, Black British feminism and resistance in education: a roundtable discussion' recounts the conference plenary discussion between Suki Ali, Senior Lecturer in Sociology at London School of Economics, Heidi Mirza, then Professor of Equalities Studies, IOE, and Director of The Centre for Rights, Equalities and Social Justice, and Ann Phoenix, Co-Director of the Thomas

Coram Research Unit, IOE, chaired by Jessica Ringrose, Senior Lecturer in Sociology of Gender and Education, IOE. The roundtable discussion touches on some of the psychosocial complexities of gender conflicts raised by Britzman, through an exploration of 'intersectional' feminist approaches that attempt to break apart any monolith, singular notion of gender by situating gender in relationship to other key 'axes' of power including, race, class, culture sexuality (etc.). The panel profiles local London-based Black feminist educational scholars, discussing the political genesis, trajectory and contemporary 'state' of Black British feminism in relation to the meanings and viability of diverse 'intersectionality' approaches, key to some Black feminist thinkers. The panel returns to a key conference theme, discussing the effects of structural versus poststructural takes on intersectionality, with the speakers accenting the importance of understanding subjective *and* social complexity, and 'to have the psychic and the social theorised together' in drawing out the meanings of 'resistances' to 'institutionalised' intersectional oppressions. The speakers discuss, for instance, how a psychosocial intersectional approach complicates how we might understand Black British girls' negotiations of educational 'achievement' or Caribbean serial migrants' reflective negotiations of school experience after arrival in the UK, through the lens of memory. Finally, the conceptual limits of 'blackness', its inclusionary and exclusionary nature as a political identity, the issues of essentialism, and postcolonial, global and transnational Black feminisms in the plural are discussed and debated by the panellists and via a stimulating question and answer period with the audience.

The fifth paper, by Silvia Grinberg, Professor of Pedagogy and Sociology of Education and Director of Centre for Contemporary Pedagogical Studies, Universidad Nacional de San Martin, 'Everyday banality in a documentary by teenage women: between the trivial and the extreme. Schooling and Desiring in Contexts of Extreme Urban Poverty', is an important contribution to the special issue, since it carries on the theme of interrogating global disparity and how to do ethically informed feminist research with teens in a school community of extreme poverty in Buenos Aires. However, the paper both takes up and extends the theoretical orientation of the conference theme on regulation and resistance (emergent as we have suggested from a Foucauldian focus on governmentality and Butlerian theories of (hetero)sexed regulations) embracing a growing trend in education to use Giles Deleuze and Felix Guattari (1972/2004, 1980/2004) to think outside dominant (structural/poststructural) conceptual tools for understanding subjectification via social regulation in any straightforward way (see for instance Semetsky 2004; Masny and Cole, forthcoming). Grinberg uses Deleuze and Guattari to think about 'affirmations of life' and 'flows of desire' in the context of her research project to re-think the terms through which we understand subjectivisation through theories of the relative 'lack' and 'need' of the subject alone. Grinberg brings to bear conceptual resources that highlight both structural understandings of power and psychical experiences of poverty. Reviewing 'official' accountings of life in poverty, from media depictions to teacher's accounts of the 'infected neighbourhood' of the slum area, Grinberg argues powerfully 'the desiring production of the people who live there, the way they actually live, is nowhere to be found in any possible imagination, narrative or display'. Grinberg analyses a film constructed by teen girls from the area, which she suggests offers a different politics of (im)perception, exposing a 'sense of affirmation'. Grinberg suggests the film's power lies in exposing the everyday banality of life, and her paper attempts to reverse a theoretical lens caught up in seeing abjection from the view of the dominant, finishing her piece with a provocative discussion centred on asking whether 'in a world where the will to nothing reins, a world of abjection, [does] the affirmation of life constitute, perhaps, an act of resistance'? She suggests that from the young women's filmic production emerges 'something that lies beyond nihilism, violence and apathy', that their reading is neither 'romantic' nor 'nihilistic' rather a 'political reading of their own living conditions' that usurps epistemic binaries: 'where one expects to see death these young women attest to life'.

Finally, we are fortunate enough to also be able to include an additional article in this special issue, 'Charting cartographies of resistance: lines of flight in women artists narratives', by Maria Tamboukou, Reader in Sociology and co-director of the Centre for Narrative Research, University of East London. Although not part of the plenary sessions, we elected to include Tamboukou's piece because it carries on some of the important theoretical debates initiated in the conference theme and in Grinberg's article, by exploring explicit connections between Foucault and Deleuze and Guattari that help us to continue to re-think what we might mean by both regulation and resistance. The paper explores the narratives of May Stevens, a working-class woman artist in Boston in the 1940s. Tamboukou works to re-figure traditional sociological understandings of marginalisation through the social axes of class and gender by exploring the 'lines of flight' or 'relations of exteriority' that escape these stratifications, through analysis of Stevens' narratives. Tamboukou suggests 'education and art should be analysed as an *assemblage*, a complex social entity where power relations and forces of desire are constantly at play in creating conditions of possibility for women to resist, imagine themselves becoming other and for new possibilities in their lives to be actualised'. She posits the methodological impetus of assemblage theory is to always map immanent connections and potentialities of resistance. Provocatively, Tamboukou suggests theorising resistance forces us to 'rethink the problem of the micro/macro relation'; in gender and education (and beyond); and her approach involves drawing upon both Foucault and Deleuze's re-thinking of a philosophy of time to help us perceive the possibilities of becoming in the present and futurity. Explicitly linking Foucault's famous theorisation that 'there are no relations of power without resistances' (Foucault 1980, 142) to Deleuzian theories of immanence, Tamboukou concludes: 'women artists' narratives trace lines of flight and recount events of becoming other. But ... leaving the self always entails the risk of reterritorialisation within new segmentarities' and what is just as important is understanding the experience of being in the middle, 'the intermezzo', in process.

Concluding thoughts

To conclude, the hope is that this special issue, which brings together key debates from the 2009 GEA themed conference on 'regulation and resistance', has highlighted some of the most pressing contemporary issues in the field of gender and education today. The articles underline the need for educational research to: attend to historical and psychosocial specificity, chart local complexity and global disparity, de-colonise our Euro-western-centered gender analysis, and consistently engage with the economic and policy domains of education as researchers and practitioners, if we want to effectively tackle the diversity and complexity of gender equality issues in education. The pieces also showcase some of the varied and wide-ranging theoretical approaches at play in current gender and education scholarship, and raise questions about the types of research methods that can open up new ways of documenting processes of social and subjective struggle and transformation in education, globally.

To my mind, then, the special issue stimulates important thinking about what has been, what is, and what can be, as we face the future of gender and educational engagement, struggle and debate.

Acknowledgements
I would like to gratefully acknowledge the support of the editors of *Gender and Education*, Debbie Epstein, Mary Jane Kehily and Emma Renold, in helping me with the production of this special issue, particularly Emma who gave me unflagging support and belief that things would eventually come together! I would also like to acknowledge Deborah Youdell's assistance in handling some of the email communications regarding the special issue. Finally, I extend a huge thanks to Miriam David for her invaluable comments and feedback on this introduction.

Notes
1. The core conference organising team included Deborah Youdell, Heidi Mirza and Veena Meetoo, and I would like to gratefully acknowledge their help and support in planning and running the conference. Special thanks also go to Elaine Unterhalter and Miriam David for their assistance during the conference in chairing keynote and plenary panel sessions, and to members of the IOE Gender and Sexuality in Education Special Interest Group, who reviewed conference abstracts.
2. Unfortunately, Grace Livingstone felt unable to contribute a paper to the special issue, in part due to the traumatic experience she suffered in relation to the conference. Although understandable, we greatly regret the absence of her paper.

References
Butler, J. 1993. *Bodies that matter: On the discursive limits of sex.* London: Routledge.
Butler, J. 1997. *The psychic life of power: Theories in subjection.* London: Routledge.
Deleuze, G., and F. Guattari. 1972/2004. *Anti-Oedipus: Capitalism and schizophrenia.* London: Continuum.
Deleuze, G., and F. Guattari. 1980/2004. *A thousand plateaus: Capitalism and schizophrenia.* Trans. and Foreword Brian Massumi. London: Continuum.
Fennell, S., and M. Arnot. 2009. Decentralizing hegemonic gender theory: the implications for educational research. RECOUP Working Paper no. 21, Development Studies and Faculty of Education, University of Cambridge.
Foucault, M. 1978/1990. *The history of sexuality: An introduction.* New York: Vintage Books.
Foucault, M. 1980 'Powers and strategies', an interview. In *Power/knowledge: Selected interviews and other writings 1972–1977*, ed. C. Gordon, 134–45. Trans. C. Gordon. London: Harvester Wheatsheaf.
Masny, D., and D.R. Cole, eds. Forthcoming. Education and the politics of becoming. Special issue, *Discourse: Studies in the Cultural Politics of Education.*
Semetsky, I. 2004. Introduction: Experiencing Deleuze. *Educational Philosophy and Theory* 36: 227–32.

Jessica Ringrose
Institute of Education, University of London

Kartini's children: on the need for thinking gender and education together on a world scale

Raewyn Connell

Faculty of Education and Social Work, University of Sydney, Sydney, Australia

> A world policy agenda for gender equality in education now exists, realising the idea of earlier reformers such as Kartini. This agenda, however, makes assumptions that are strongly contested by research and policy debates in national forums. This essay urges shifting the framework of gender analysis to global scale. It outlines what is involved in thinking about gender as a worldwide structure, and reconstructing gender theory to include the intellectual work of the global periphery. It explores problems in theorising education on a world scale, as a process deeply linked with gender, and related dilemmas in policy thinking. Finally, it offers suggestions about the role of researchers on gender and education, and the importance of building an educational case for gender justice.

The shape of the problem
Kartini and the Millennium

About a hundred years ago a young woman in Java, then under the colonial rule of the Netherlands, conceived a plan of educational reform. Kartini was critical of the marginalisation of women in the ruling-class Muslim community she lived in. She found a way to get in touch with progressive intellectuals in the colonising power, especially her pen-friend Stella Zeehandelaar. She decided to opt out of the usual life path of arranged marriage and motherhood, to become a writer, and to start a reform process by founding a school for women.

As it turned out, she could not get financial backing from the colonial state to do teacher training or to start her school, so she didn't become a headmistress. Her family desired her to enter a proper marriage, and she complied. Kartini died of complications of her first childbirth, in 1904.

But her story didn't end there. She was indeed a writer. Her letters to Stella were published, and became a classic of colonial literature (Kartini 2005). In time, Kartini became a heroine of the Indonesian independence movement, and has remained an icon in the story of Indonesian women's organisations (Robinson 2009).

A hundred years later, the United Nations formulated another plan for women's education, in the Millennium Development Goals (MDG) adopted in the year 2000 CE. MDG 2 was to *achieve universal primary education*, with the specific target to ensure that all boys and girls complete a full course of primary schooling. MDG 3 was to *promote gender equality and empower women*, with the target to eliminate gender disparity in primary and secondary education preferably by 2005, and at all levels by 2015. Ratios of girls to boys in school enrolments, and ratio of literate women to men, were among the indicators for this Goal.

Modest these goals are, in relation to a full understanding of gender equality (Unterhalter 2007, 14–15). Yet if they were actually achieved, they would amount to the biggest gender equity initiative in the history of the world.

Governments are not currently on track to meet the goals in all countries, and the global recession will have made the task harder. Even so, the Millennium Development Goals, in combination with the UNESCO-coordinated Education For All agenda (UNESCO 2003), demonstrate a remarkable shift since the time of Kartini. The colonial state said 'no' to her, but the postcolonial state is now saying 'yes' to her project.

The education of girls and women is now almost universally recognised as a public responsibility. States maintain massive institutional systems, i.e. schools, colleges and universities, and employ massive workforces, to perform this task. The achievement of gender equality in education is an explicit goal, at least in principle, of every government in the world. The 'leap to equality', as UNESCO calls it, is happening on an enormous scale.

Categorical policy and local research

It feels ungenerous, therefore, to be critical of this global policy. But these formulations by international bodies represent a *type* of policy which has been subject to important criticisms at the national or local level. Drawing on these debates, we can identify three key assumptions of current international gender-equality policy.

First, policy documents about gender almost always take 'women' and 'girls', on the one side, and 'men' and 'boys' on the other, as fixed, unproblematic categories. Statistical measures of difference between such categories are the stock in trade of policy argument. Indeed, as Schofield (2004) puts it for health policy, the statistical margin of difference between the categories effectively *becomes* the meaning of 'gender'. There is a powerful process of regulation here, which obliterates differences within categories; and marginalises the issues that have come to be called 'intersectionality', about the interaction of gender with class and race. Yet we must acknowledge that only through categorical arguments have state elites been persuaded to adopt gender policies at all.

Second, categorical policy about gender equality in education takes formal schooling as an unquestioned good. Justice is thought to be achieved simply by providing more of it to an underrepresented group. Specifically, it is assumed by most policy-makers that schooling is gender-neutral, and having more of it will 'empower women'. Complexities are acknowledged in the more sophisticated official documents, especially the very good 2003 UNESCO report *Gender and Education for All*. Yet the overall policy drive of state elites is simply to expand the school and college system, with curriculum and pedagogy taken for granted. This is consistent with the logic of mechanical economic development and enrichment so bitterly apparent at the 2009 Copenhagen climate summit.

Third, it is typical of categorical gender policy that it targets women and girls, and includes men and boys only in a shadow sense. Men and boys figure as the statistical norm against which the position of women and girls is measured, or as the perpetrators (in policy about violence or harassment), or generally as the holders of privilege. They have not, until very recently, figured as the subjects of gender equity policy or as actors in gender change (Connell 2005).

Each of these assumptions of categorical gender policy in education has now been seriously challenged. National policy debates, such as the 'Promoting Gender Equity' conference in Australia more than a decade ago (Gender Equity Taskforce 1995), have argued for a different framing of issues. Developments in gender theory have called categoricalism sharply into question. The neglect of issues about boys and men allowed an essentialist backlash discourse to gain traction. There is now a shift in international policy thinking about this, as narrated in the recent UN document on the role of men and boys in achieving gender equality (Division for the Advancement of Women 2008).

These questionings have been influenced by several decades of close-focus research on gender, youth and schooling, using interviews, ethnographies, autobiographies, and thematic analysis of texts. The studies published in forums such as *Gender and Education* have shown in great detail that gender patterns are not fixed, that identities are negotiated in individual lives and categories emerge historically, that masculinities and femininities are multiple, and that gender relations vary in different class, ethnic and national contexts. (To cite only one example from a very rich literature, all these points are evidenced in the splendid study of London teenage boys by Frosh, Phoenix, and Pattman 2002.) In short, gender is a complex dynamic structure, not a simple, natural dichotomy. Schooling, in turn, is far from gender-neutral. When we look at a school playground or an education system, we are looking at a writhing mass of gender effects. And boys and men are right in the fray – not background, not in the shadows, but as deeply enmeshed in gender processes as are women and girls.

This research has been wonderfully creative, and we would have a poor understanding of gender and education without it. Yet the great majority of the studies published in journals such as *Gender and Education*, whatever country they come from, have a local focus, and also have an *intellectual* framing that is internal to the global North. Colleagues such as Heward and Bunwaree (1999), Unterhalter (2007) and Arnot (2009) have now urged us to do something different: to do research-informed thinking about gender, education, citzenship and justice on a world scale.

It is vital that their invitation be accepted. Researchers cannot think straight about school ethnographies or youth surveys if they treat the research site as sitting at the bottom of a silo. Conversely, policymakers cannot think straight about the global equity agenda without connecting to the genres of research that have been so fruitful at a local level. But how can we bring educational research, theory and gender equality policy together on a world scale? That is a vast project, and will need the work of many hands. In this essay, drawing on the work of many scholars, I outline an approach that may be useful.

Conceptualising gender on a world scale
Colonisation and globalisation as a gender dynamic

Despite popular theories of globalisation that picture us 'all in the same boat now', we are not. World society involves structured systems of inequality, growing out of a 500-year history of violence, conquest and economic subordination. Most of the world's people live in societies that have experienced colonial or semi-colonial conditions in the past and neo-colonial domination or marginality since.

The history of a world-spanning imperial order is a gendered history. The surge of power that laid hold of lands and societies, transforming local cultures and integrating local economies into global capitalism, also laid hold of local gender orders. In the trauma of conquest or enslavement these might be torn apart; even in the most benign cases they were subject to disintegrating pressures.

To give some examples: in many parts of the world the men of colonised societies were taken away to provide the labour of plantations or mines, as slave labour, indentured labour, or cheap wage labour (Jayawardena 1963). Women's and men's traditional relations to the land were transformed by the imposition of colonial property law (Stauffer 2004). Women's labour was transformed by the advent of wage labour for men and a housewife model for women (Mies 1986). The legendary stories that gave local ethical guidance for gender relations were attacked as superstition (but are now being reaffirmed: Bell 2008). Gender categories or practices offensive to colonising Christianity were attacked; for instance the 'berdache' or two-souled people of south-western North America were destroyed with brutality by Spanish colonialism (Williams 1986).

Colonised peoples of course resisted, and when resistance failed, they adjusted to changed circumstances. So the history of the destruction of gender orders is also the history of the creation of new gender arrangements. Some were highly inventive, such as the 'mine marriages' and 'women with manhood' created around South African gold mining (Moodie and Ndatshe 1994). During the twentieth century, the resistance of the colonised finally led to de-colonisation on a large scale; but the pressure for gender change did not end with political independence.

Much of the de-colonised world entered new relationships of cultural and economic dependence. Developmentalist states, from Latin America to India and China, followed the lead of Japan in trying to industrialise, creating another kind of masculinised labour force. Most post-colonial states maintained masculinised European-style armies, many of which became the dominant force in local affairs. Women, meanwhile, were increasingly drawn into the money economy in subordinate roles, a process that has accelerated dramatically worldwide in the last few decades. As development economics and neoliberal market ideology gained influence, women were increasingly perceived by policymakers as an untapped labour force and as bearers of human capital. This gave a rationale for women's education, and was compatible with the formal equality enshrined in human rights documents.

Since capitalist development both undermined traditional patriarchies and generated new forms of gender inequality, it is necessary to go beyond the tradition-versus-modernity dichotomy that is still influential in gender debates. Gender is an embedded feature of the new global economy (Peterson 2003). But the gender relations are geographically dispersed, as transnational corporations assemble a jigsaw of exploitation of gendered labour – data entry by women here, microprocessor assembly by women there, trucking by men somewhere else, and so on. The marketing of global goods and services depends on mutations of gender imagery, from glossy fashion magazines to powdered milk sales. New patterns of gendered sexuality, from North American sex tourism in the Caribbean to the multiple partners of long-distance truck drivers in Africa, have been traced as pathways of HIV transmission in the AIDS epidemic.

The new institutions and arenas of globalisation are themselves gendered, in the sense that they have evolving gender regimes. Transnational management, the international state, global media and global markets all have gender patterns and most of them involve stark gender inequalities. The top levels of management in transnational companies are practically monopolised by men (for instance, men made up 98% of CEOs in the 2007 count of *Fortune* magazine's 'Global 500' corporations). The forms of masculinity constructed in transnational business are beginning to be researched (Olavarría 2009). It is important to recognise, as we think about global gender equality policy, that the states and inter-state bodies that make such policies are overwhelmingly controlled by men; and that in a neoliberal world, these states are interlocked with the management of transnational corporations.

Theory trouble

In this swelling scene of gender transformations, how do we theorise gender? The massive worldwide reform agenda in education, while certainly resulting from the sustained efforts of feminists, has been formulated with little input from feminist theory. We might almost say it has been formulated in opposition to feminist theory. For two decades gender theory in the global metropole,[1] especially the USA and UK, has been led by a school of thought whose key move was to criticise the assumption that 'women' could be taken as a well-founded category.

Deconstructionism, and the closely allied interpretation of gender as a discursive accomplishment, has focused attention on the performative utterances and actions by which people constitute themselves as gendered, and on the discursive norms that regulate this performative process. This does not give much grip on the institutions that gender equity policy deals with. A fairly recent textbook on gender theory that highlights post-structuralist thought does not have a single index entry for the 'state', 'education', 'economy' or 'children' (Alsop, Fitzsimons, and Lennon 2002).

Deconstructionist gender theory focuses on processes of regulation understood as normativity. The creative moment in which gender is performatively brought into being is understood as the action of the individual; and resistance involves brave individual departures from norms. North American queer politics, operating along these lines, challenges the norms even of lesbian and gay communities. This has been an attractive model for young activists in many countries. It has valorised gender diversity, and led to a kind of radical tolerance or inclusiveness which is an important renovating force for feminism.

But with such a conception of power and of radical action, it is difficult to generate the idea of a policy process that involves collective action and institution-building. Indeed that seems inherently normalising, and hence subject to the persistent critique of normativity – even if it is a new norm that is being introduced.

But there are forms of feminism and theorisations of gender which are not afraid of normativity (Johnson 1994; Jónasdóttir 1994). The emergence of a feminist theory of citizenship offers a different conception of political power, in gender terms (Arnot 2009).

Further, while deconstructionism has been hegemonic in the global metropole, normative concerns have been central for feminism in the global periphery. Feminism in India, for instance, has been heavily committed in struggles and research around the prevention of violence – rape, domestic violence, dowry deaths, public violence in communalism and caste oppression (Purkayastha et al. 2009). Feminism in South Africa gained normative commitments to equality from the post-Apartheid state, including the most progressive equality guarantees in the world written into the 1996 Constitution; and has struggled to turn this into economic and social reality. Feminism in Latin America, re-surfacing after the dictatorships and the economic catastrophe of the 1980s, has developed a sophisticated methodology for holding governments to their normative commitments on gender issues (Valdés 2001).

So the problem that Mohanty (2003) calls 'decolonizing theory' is an important conceptual problem, not just a diplomatic one. The hegemony of the metropole is part of what feminist theory should be analysing, as part of what we understand by gender itself. Mies' *Patriarchy and Accumulation on a World Scale* (1986) can be seen in retrospect as a pioneering theorisation of the mutual constitution of gender and colonialism.

The hegemony of the metropole is a tangible reality for researchers everywhere else in the world. When Kartini looked to the colonial power for help and inspiration, she was doing what intellectuals in the periphery have constantly done. For good reasons: the concentration of wealth and organisational resources at the imperial centre; the global flow of information into metropolitan institutions (universities, museums, research institutes); the concentration of the means of publication and publicity (journals, book companies, etc.); the programmes of research training; and now the Internet, global in promise but firmly centred on the USA.

These processes constitute a global political economy of knowledge. In this economy, knowledge production in the periphery takes the form that the Beninese philosopher Hountondji (1997) calls 'extraversion'. The periphery becomes a source of data, and a site of application, while the concentration of data and the moment of theorising occurs in the metropole. Therefore intellectuals living in the periphery are strongly oriented to the metropole.

But there are also counter-forces. Hountondji and his colleagues have explored 'endogenous knowledge' in west Africa and its complex relationship with the sciences of the metropole. Smith (1999), on the basis of Maori experience in Aotearoa/New Zealand, has argued for 'decolonizing methodologies'. Feminists are now very familiar with the idea that different feminisms arise in different regions of the world.

In *Re-orienting Western Feminisms* Bulbeck (1998) has addressed the epistemological consequences of rejecting the hegemony of the metropole, i.e. contesting extraversion in gender politics and theory. It isn't comfortable. Oyěwùmí (1997) has even argued that, in the context of Yoruba society in west Africa, the very concept of 'woman' as a social category was introduced by colonialism, so feminism as such is neo-colonial. But this view is contested by other Yoruba scholars; who argue also that African cultures have always been open to cultural exchange (Bakare-Yusuf 2003). Bulbeck proposes a nuanced relativism as the path forward. It involves a practice she calls 'braiding at the borderlands', an endless negotiation among differing positions to create the possibilities of communication and action.

Theory can no longer be a monologue. It is no longer adequate to conceptualise gender in a way that reflects only the concerns of the global metropole, or of a group within the metropole. We need, rather, what might be called negotiated theory, that acknowledges the world's multiple experiences of gender issues, and builds on the differing intellectual traditions and contemporary efforts at understanding around the globe. This is hard to do and the products will often be awkward amalgams and compromises. But we have to try.

Conceptualising education on a world scale
The interplay of education with gender
Gender theorists in the metropole have usually had little to say about education, instead developing their concepts of gender by thinking about sexuality, symbolism or

(in an older style) the economy. Gender researchers in education therefore have usually conceived their task as studying 'gender and education' as a conjunction of two distinct things; and policymakers in education have been able to treat gender equity policy as an optional add-on to their real business.

I think we have been too modest. Gender researchers in education can make larger intellectual claims – indeed, should develop arguments about the nature of education itself. This becomes more intelligible, indeed more urgent, when we think about the issue on a world scale.

Educational processes are about the development of human capacities for practice, both individual and social. If this sounds like a statement in human capital theory, that does not mean it is mistaken – human capital theory is not wrong, it is just emotionally stunted. Education involves the development of capacities across the full range of human practices (as the creators of the original 'core curriculum' idea argued). This range includes housework, emotional expression and control, child care, artistry, relationship building, and the body-reflexive practices by which gender is constituted.

Education is, therefore, integral to gender; it concerns the moment in social process when people as agents enter the historical constitution of gender relations. The feminists of an earlier generation had a sound insight when they criticised conventional sex-role socialisation, though we can now see severe limits in their theoretical language.

On the other hand, educational processes, being coordinated social practices, are shaped by the social structures that organise societies, and one of those structures is gender. Where there is a gender division of labour in infant and child care, there is necessarily a gender structuring of early childhood education. Where there is a gender ordering of employment and authority in the state, there is necessarily a gender structuring of education in public school systems. Where families are structured around gender difference, the interactions between families and schools are necessarily gender-structured.

The mass school systems created in the metropole during the nineteenth century, as Miller (1998) shows, were part of a vast social transformation which replaced the old household-centred patriarchalism with a new gender order involving bureaucratic state institutions, a separation of the capitalist economy from the household, and the removal of children from productive labour. It is not surprising that school systems were born segregated, nor that education in the metropole continues to be gender-structured, in the changing ways richly documented by modern research (Arnot, David, and Weiner 1999; Frank and Davidson 2007).

The conventional assumption about the global history of schooling is that modern school systems were invented in 'the West', i.e. the imperial metropole, and were implanted after colonisation in the course of the West's civilising mission. Ruling elites in Japan and Turkey installed them without the aid of a colonising power, and thus sought to enter the circle of modernity.

This story has to be modified. School systems were constructed in the colonies at much the same time as they were being developed in the metropole. Education was not a colonial afterthought, but an important component of what Mudimbe (1994) calls the 'colonizing apparatus' that re-shaped economy, power and culture. This is illustrated by his historical study of Mpala village in the eastern Congo, where elementary schooling – but no more than elementary – was part of a total reorganisation of local society that subordinated it to the colonisers. Colonisation everywhere involved disruption of local social structures and practices, including local practices for the education of children. The course of events was different, but the result as profound as the transformation of patriarchy in the metropole.

This disruption continues under the aegis of development and modernisation. Aikman's (1999) research with the Arakmbut people of Amazonian Peru provides a striking illustration of the contemporary process by which the school system managed by a modernising state and an evangelising church disrupts indigenous knowledge and re-orders gender relations. The course of events that Aikman describes, the imposition of an alien knowledge system which the children are compelled to learn, is a striking denial of curricular justice (Connell 1993). It parallels the experience in Canada, the USA, New Zealand and Australia where small-scale indigenous communities, displaced or fragmented by settler colonialism, are also marginalised in post-colonial school systems.

There is a broader principle here, which also applies to education in post-colonial countries with indigenous majorities. The creation of a mass school system and the installation of a hegemonic academic curriculum is an example of what the Brazilian social theorist Domingues (2008) calls a 'modernizing offensive'. In creating new institutions the offensive creates new relations of marginality and privilege. Part of the process is the creation of a gendered workforce, through mechanisms such as the *Escolas Normais*, the teacher training institutions for women, in Brazil. Despite subordination in the workplace, the possession of privileged forms of knowledge gives a certain cultural and economic leverage to the women involved. Thus the expansion of school systems by post-colonial states widely becomes a dynamic of change in gender relations.

The latest modernising offensive in education is the agenda of global neoliberalism. Agencies such as the World Bank and the OECD have spread the gospel of free markets, privatisation and competition, which has had complex but strong effects on education systems. Among them is the elaboration of 'league tables' for schools, universities, indeed countries (via international testing programmes). Here a technology of educational measurement originally intended for research has mutated into an apparatus of competition, supposed to provide consumer information to families purchasing educational services in a market.

Many educational processes have been commodified in the course of this offensive, and some global markets have been created. But the rationing of education that is necessary to create market competition (Gillborn and Youdell 2000) means that benefits are concentrated among privileged social groups. In broad terms, neoliberal education has fostered the creation of a global middle class. Though market ideology presents itself as gender-neutral, this dynamic is strongly gendered. One effect is to create a new role for middle-class women as 'education mothers' (as they are called in Japan), pulling out all stops to promote their children's progress through a competitive education system. Research in Kolkata has described the breathtaking recent expansion of private English-language pre-schools in a developing mega-city, with heavy involvement of middle-class mothers, and the re-shaping of family life around the task of projecting children, especially boys, into the global white-collar labour market (Donner 2006).

The modernising offensive of neoliberalism has different effects in other contexts. A recent report by Morrell (2007), 'On a knife's edge: masculinity in Black working-class schools in post-Apartheid education', decribes masculinity formation in the aftermath of a struggle in which Black male youth were formerly the spearhead. The ANC's turn to neoliberalism, in a context of massive racial and class inequalities in

South Africa, has left the state and its school system unable to hold the loyalty of many male youth in poor communities. Gangs have formed and sexual violence is widespread. There are, however, many youth who resist this solution, or who are ambivalent in their support for it. Morrell points to other masculinities, to wider community disapproval of the gangs, and to the spreading influence of discourses of racial and gender equality, in opening other possibilities.

Policy trouble

The 'Women in Development' movement of the 1970s roundly criticised post-independence aid programmes for failing to recognise women's agricultural work. Feminists tried to build programmes specifically targeted to rural women, and to make sure that a share of increasing productivity actually went to women. In the late 1980s and 1990s this was challenged by a 'Gender and Development' perspective, that emphasised the way gender is built into economic and domestic institutions, requiring a broader contestation of patriarchy. This too, as Heward and Bunwaree (1999) point out, rested on a categorical understanding of gender; and applied to education, led to a focus on the statistical gender gap and measures to close it. So did the World Bank approach based on human-capital thinking, which saw investment in girls' education as a key strategy for economic development.

Morrell's study of boys, and most of the research with girls and women in Heward and Bunwaree's volume, rest on a relational view of gender. Multiple masculinities and femininities may come into existence. Forms of gender, and groups and alliances defined in gender relations, are produced in a historical process which, as in South Africa, can be very conflictual. There is not a fixed gender hierarchy; rival patriarchies may lay claim to power, and new strategies of resistance or reform may emerge. Schools and school systems have embedded gender politics in their curriculum, their organisation, their routines and their community relations, as Morrell (2001) has shown in a superb historical study of colonial schools.

The gender dynamics of the state now come into view as part of the story of education. In a celebrated article Stromquist (1995) analysed the feminist practice of 'romancing the state', seeking educational reform by sweet persuasion of reluctant governments. Stromquist observed a hierarchy in what governments generally do for gender equity: readily committing to equal access, much less willingly taking steps that would transform schools, and least of all changing the gender content of the curriculum.

In some circumstances, a developmentalist state will invest substantially in girls' education. An instructive case is Malaysia, where a corrupt post-colonial state, controlled by ethnic Malays, markedly improved the educational situation of Malay girls – but not ethnic Chinese or Indian girls (Pong 1999).

Even where there is investment, however, we have to question a project of equality that relies on school systems as they are. Equality in exposure to a pedagogy that disrupts indigenous knowledge and gender relations? Equality in exposure to an institution that is controlled by men and embeds patriarchal rules and values? Equal presence in schools marked by violence among boys and sexual harassment of girls? Without close attention to the content of education, to curricular justice, and to sheer safety, an agenda of equality risks becoming a new format for oppression.

And yet – it is also true in the colonial world, as in the metropole, that deeply unjust education systems have provided means for women's autonomy. That was the basis of Kartini's strategy. A contemporary of Kartini's, my great-aunt Maud Connell (whom I knew as a very old woman) grew up in colonial Victoria and was one of the first women to get a university education in Australia. Maud read seven languages, never married, became a headmistress, and inspired other women and men in the teaching trade. Her family was part of the settler population in the British colonisation of Australia. Aboriginal women, who in Maud's day were totally marginalised, have increasingly been able to use the school and university system to gain access to knowledge and jobs. It has been a painfully slow process, but a measure of curricular justice for indigenous students is creeping into Australian schools (Foley 2010).

It seems that formal schooling, and the equality agenda, form an arena that we cannot abandon. The problem is not only to gain equal access, but to build on equal access, to use that as a platform for work on institutions and curricula.

Researchers and the arena of gender justice

What role can researchers play on this political terrain? Research often seems remote from the day-to-day struggles for peace, justice, land, and survival. By the time a good project is designed, funded, put into the field, nursed through its crises, finished, written up and published, years have usually gone by and the battle is being fought on other ground. Nevertheless, democratic movements have needs for knowledge, and well-thought-out research is the cutting edge of knowledge production.

An orientation to gender equality is essential for gender researchers; that is what makes our work responsible, in the current policy environment. At the same time, research can feed new understandings into the political process around gender equality.

Research has made clear that 'gender equality' is not a simple target. The gender orders revealed by research contain multiple structures. The gender practices are frequently contradictory, and the processes of change are turbulent. The Latin American index of achievement of gender commitments is exemplary; progress towards gender justice must be measured in multiple directions at once (Valdés 2001). It follows that gender equality policy does not involve just one mechanism and one goal. Quantitative programmes such as the Millennium Development Goals do matter, but should not be thought the whole story.

Research certainly helped to thematise men's involvement in gender change, gender dynamics among men and boys, the multiplicity of masculinities, and the political possibilities they open up. Policy frameworks for men and boys' involvement now exist (Varanka, Närhinen and Siukola 2006; Division for the Advancement of Women 2008). This is one of the most important changes in the policy arena in the last two decades, and gender researchers share the credit for making it happen.

Educational justice concerns not only the amount of education but also what is learnt and the way knowledge functions in social processes. A good deal of what gender researchers discover about schools concerns the effects of the hidden curriculum; gender determinations are also important in the official curriculum. This is the area in which, as Stromquist (1995) observed, commitments have been hardest to get from governments. We might think of curricular justice as the frontier of global gender equity in education.

I think it very important that gender researchers should stay in the arena of policy. To repeat, feminisms in the world periphery mostly do have a strongly normative character. In relation to curriculum, the most brilliant critique of gender effects is not enough; it is necessary to enter debates about what the curriculum ought to be, and how it can be realised in classrooms. Having cleaned the kitchen, we need to share in the baking.

Specifically, this means thinking about what capacities for practice are needed for a gender-just world, and how educational processes might produce them. A notable example of such thinking is the attempt to produce a 'socially inclusive curriculum' for the Victorian Certificate of Education (the high school graduation certificate), proposed by the most influential feminist educator in Australian history, Jean Blackburn (Ministerial Review of Postcompulsory Schooling, Victoria 1985).

The case for gender justice in education has often been made on the basis of 'rights'. The global agenda in education can draw on a tradition of international rights statements, from the Universal Declaration of Human Rights, to the Convention on the Elimination of All Forms of Discrimination Against Women, to the Declaration of the Rights of the Child. Yet ultimately, the case has to be an educational one, reflecting ideas of what makes good education. Good education is education that is just; the quality of education is defined by the quality of social life generated by the capacities that education yields.

In that sense we will never be in a post-feminist educational situation where gender policy is no longer needed, because the production of a gender-equal social world is a continuing process. Activism, and the research that supports it, will continue to be needed for a just and survivable world.

Acknowledgements

This paper is based on a keynote address to 'Regulation and Resistance', the conference of the Gender and Education Association, London, 25–27 March 2009. I am grateful to organisers and participants for the opportunity to be there and for the lively discussions that occurred.

Note

1. By 'metropole' I mean the group of capital-rich countries in North America and Europe, many of them former imperialist powers, that form the core of the global economy, have predominant military power and cultural hegemony. The global 'periphery' includes the poorest countries and regions, but also includes rich countries with dependent economies that are products of settler colonialism, including Australia and New Zealand. The relationships between these groups are historically dynamic, not fixed.

References

Aikman, Sheila. 1999. Schooling and development: Eroding Amazon women's knowledge and diversity. In *Gender, education and development: Beyond access to empowerment*, ed. Christine Heward and Sheila Bunwaree, 65–81. London: Zed Books.
Alsop, Rachel, Annette Fitzsimons, and Kathleen Lennon. 2002. *Theorizing gender*. Cambridge: Polity.
Arnot, Madeleine. 2009. *Educating the gendered citizen: Sociological engagements with national and global agendas*. Abingdon, UK: Routledge.
Arnot, Madeleine, Miriam David, and Gaby Weiner. 1999. *Closing the gender gap: Postwar education and social change*. Cambridge: Polity Press.
Bakare-Yusuf, Bibi. 2003. 'Yorubas don't do gender': a critical review of Oyeronke Oyewumi's *The Invention of Women: Making an African Sense of Western Gender Discourses*. *African Identities* 1: 121–43.
Bell, Diane, ed. 2008. *Kungun Ngarrindjeri Miminar Yunnan: Listen to Ngarrindjeri women speaking*. Melbourne: Spinifex Press.

Bulbeck, Chilla. 1998. *Re-orienting western feminisms: Women's diversity in a postcolonial world.* Cambridge: Cambridge University Press.

Connell, Raewyn. 1993. *Schools and social justice.* Philadelphia: Temple University Press.

Connell, Raewyn. 2005. Change among the gatekeepers: Men, masculinities, and gender equality in the global arena. *Signs* 30: 1801–25.

Division for the Advancement of Women (United Nations). 2008. *The role of men and boys in achieving gender equality.* 'Women 2000 and Beyond' series. New York: Division for the Advancement of Women, Department of Economic and Social Affairs, United Nations.

Domingues, José Maurício. 2008. *Latin America and contemporary modernity: A sociological interpretation.* New York: Routledge.

Donner, Henrike. 2006. Committed mothers and well-adjusted children: Privatisation, early-years education and motherhood in Calcutta. *Modern Asian Studies* 40: 371–95.

Foley, Dennis. 2010. Aboriginality and pedagogies. In *Education, change & society,* second edition, eds. Raewyn Connell, Craig Campbell, Margaret Vickers, Anthony Welch, Dennis Foley, Niger Bagnall and Debra Hayes, 168–704. Melbourne: Oxford University Press.

Frank, Blye W., and Kevin G. Davison, ed. 2007. *Masculinities and schooling: International practices and perspectives.* London, Canada: Althouse Press.

Frosh, Stephen, Ann Phoenix, and Rob Pattman. 2002. *Young masculinities: Understanding boys in contemporary society.* Basingstoke, UK: Palgrave.

Gender Equity Taskforce of the Ministerial Council for Education, Employment, Training and Youth Affairs. 1995. *Proceedings of the Promoting Gender Equity Conference.* Canberra: ACT Department of Education and Training.

Gillborn, David, and Deborah Youdell. 2000. *Rationing education: Policy, practice, reform and equity.* Buckingham, UK: Open University Press.

Heward, Christine, and Sheila Bunwaree, ed. 1999. *Gender, education and development: Beyond access to empowerment.* London: Zed Books.

Hountondji, Paulin J. 1997. Introduction: Recentring Africa. In *Endogenous knowledge: Research trails,* ed. Paulin J. Hountondji, 1–39. Dakar: CODESRIA.

Jayawardena, Chandra. 1963. *Conflict and solidarity in a Guianese plantation.* London: Athlone Press.

Johnson, Pauline. 1994. *Feminism as radical humanism.* Sydney: Allen & Unwin.

Jónasdóttir, Anna G. 1994. *Why women are oppressed.* Philadelphia: Temple University Press.

Kartini. 2005. *On feminism and nationalism: Kartini's letters to Stella Zeehandelaar, 1899–1903.* Melbourne: Monash University Press.

Mies, Maria. 1986. *Patriarchy and accumulation on a world scale.* London: Zed Books.

Miller, Pavla. 1998. *Transformations of patriarchy in the West, 1500–1900.* Bloomington: Indiana University Press.

Ministerial Review of Postcompulsory Schooling, Victoria. 1985. *Report.* Melbourne: Ministerial Review.

Mohanty, Chandra Talpade. 2003. *Feminism without borders: Decolonizing theory, practicing solidarity.* Durham, NC: Duke University Press.

Moodie, T. Dunbar, with Vivienne Ndatshe. 1994. *Going for gold: Men, mines and migration.* Johannesburg: Witwatersrand University Press.

Morrell, Robert. 2001. *From boys to gentlemen: Settler masculinity in colonial Natal 1880–1920.* Pretoria: University of South Africa.

Morrell, Robert. 2007. On a knife's edge: Masculinity in Black working-class schools in post-Apartheid education. In *Masculinities and schooling: International practices and perspectives,* ed. Blye W. Frank and Kevin G. Davison, 35–57. London, Canada: Althouse Press.

Mudimbe, V.Y. 1994. *The idea of Africa.* Bloomington: Indiana University Press.

Olavarría, José, ed. 2009. *Masculinidad/es y globalización: trabajo y vida privada, Familia/s y sexualidad/es, V Encuentro de Estudios de Masculinidades.* Santiago, Chile: CEDEM.

Oyěwùmí, Oyèrónké. 1997. *The invention of women: Making an African sense of western gender discourses.* Minneapolis: University of Minnesota Press.

Peterson, V. Spike. 2003. *A critical rewriting of global political economy: Integrating reproductive, productive and virtual economies.* London: Routledge.

Pong, Suet-ling. 1999. Gender inequality in educational attainment in peninsular Malaysia. In *Gender, education and development: Beyond access to empowerment,* ed. Christine Heward and Sheila Bunwaree, 155–70. London: Zed Books.

Purkayastha, Bandana, Mangala Subramaniam, Manisha Desai, and Sunita Bose. 2009. The study of gender in India: A partial review. In *Global gender research: Transnational perspectives,* ed. Christine E. Bose and Minjeong Kim, 92–109. New York: Routledge.
Robinson, Kathryn. 2009. *Gender, Islam and democracy in Indonesia.* London: Routledge.
Schofield, Toni. 2004. Boutique health: Gender and equity in health policy. Australian Health Policy Institute, Commissioned Paper Series 2004/08, The University of Sydney, Sydney.
Smith, Linda Tuhiwai. 1999. *Decolonizing methodologies: Research and indigenous peoples.* London: Zed Books.
Stauffer, Robert H. 2004. *Kahana: How the land was lost.* Honolulu: University of Hawai'i Press.
Stromquist, Nelly P. 1995. Romancing the state: Gender and power in education. *Comparative Education Review* 39: 423–54.
UNESCO. 2003. *Gender and education for all: The leap to equality.* Paris: UNESCO Publishing.
Unterhalter, Elaine. 2007. *Gender, schooling and global social justice.* London, Routledge.
Valdés, Teresa, ed. 2001. *El Indice de Compromiso Cumplido – ICC: Una estrategia para el control cuidadano de la equidad de género.* Santiago: FLACSO-Chile.
Varanka, Jouni, Antti Närhinen, and Reetta Siukola, eds. 2006. *Men and gender equality: Towards progressive policies.* Helsinki: Ministry of Social Affairs and Health.
Williams, Walter L. 1986. *The spirit and the flesh: Sexual diversity in American Indian culture.* Boston: Beacon Press.

Resisting dominant discourses: implications of indigenous, African feminist theory and methods for gender and education research

Bagele Chilisa[a] and Gabo Ntseane[b]

[a]Department of Educational Foundations, University of Botswana, Gaborone, Botswana;
[b]Department of Adult Education, University of Botswana, Gaborone, Botswana

> In this paper we explore tensions between Western gender theory and research, and post-colonial and indigenous feminist standpoints, which challenge us to re-define our roles as feminist-activist educators and researchers working with formerly colonised and historically marginalised communities. We discuss how African and Black feminist approaches can enable the construction of context-specific knowledge of African women's power via relational world views of motherhood, family, sisterhood and friendship. In contrast, the application of Western gender theory and policy in Botswana has tended to reduce women and girls' experiences to the categories of 'victim' and 'other'. We illustrate how Western male hegemony enters the school through subjects such as religion and can be typically reinforced through Tswana culture, embodied in language and rituals, generating multiple centres of oppression for girls/women in the education system and the public space. The paper explores ethical and transformative ways of approaching this complexity that can account for how girls and women negotiate and resist patriarchal power. Through analysis of empirical research narratives from several gender- and education-focused studies, we explore strategies for decolonising Euro-Western archival knowledge and challenging dominant, patriarchal, colonial research methodologies. Finally, we outline the role of the activist feminist researcher as transformative healer, who resists dominant research discourses in order to develop processes of social justice and healing in the community.

Introduction

This paper's theme of gender, regulation, resistance and activism calls on educators and researchers to debate the universal application of a Western gender theory and gender research in the field of education across nations and cultures. The main argument, from the vantage of non-Western feminists, is that hegemonic Western gender theory and gender research 'recreate its own knowledge in distant geographies in its own image' (Fennell and Arnot 2009, 3). These hegemonic forms of knowledge production undermine localised knowledge about education and the school systems and the accumulated literature from scholars writing from post-colonial and indigenous standpoints. We challenge universalised Western gender theory and employ post-colonial, indigenous and

African feminist approaches to reveal local standpoints that express girls'/women's agency and resistance to often contradictory forms of patriarchal oppressions. We begin with an overview of the debate in gender theory and gender research.

Gender theory and research: indigenous and African feminisms and methodologies

Fennell and Arnot (2009) have outlined four contested themes that emerge from a comparison of gender education theory from Western Europe and America and those from locations within Africa and South Asia. The first theme is an argument by non-Western feminists for a deconstruction of universalisation within gender theory. Scholars are, for instance, expressing their criticism about deficit theories on non-Western societies, omissions of their world views and oral literatures that inform their frames of reference. One of the leading scholars from the so-called third world, Mohatany (1991) points to 'othering' ideologies as a serious constraint to how non-Western people are heard and written about. The term 'othering' was coined by Gayatri Spivak to denote a process through which Western knowledge creates differences between itself as the norm and other knowledge systems as inferior (Ashcroft, Griffiths, and Tiffin 1991). There is, for instance, a discontent among non-Western feminists that some Western feminisms have used Western female-based structures of language, concepts, theories and models of reality and world views as a criteria against which experiences of all non-Western women as well as non-Western men can be known and written about. Fennell and Arnot (2009) note that the result of universalised Western gender theory is that the diversity of experiences of girls/women within formerly colonised and historically marginalised societies, their struggles, negotiations and resistance to different forms of patriarchal oppressions and domination as well as imperial domination, are most likely to go unrecognised. In this article we move out of the cage of universalised Western gender theory and employ postcolonial and indigenous standpoints to reveal local standpoints that express girls/women agency and resistance to patriarchal oppression.

The second theme centres on the denial by Western feminists of African women's power within indigenous relational worlds that celebrate motherhood, sisterhood and friendship. The variety of African feminisms in contrast to other feminisms emphasise the centrality of motherhood in African households and family organisation and the agency and power of mothers as the source of solidarity. Unfortunately, the othering of motherhood and the denial of the importance African relational gender roles, it is argued, relegates the African women to subject/victim and further conceals how girls/women have used the relational gender roles as sites for resistance and sources of empowerment. These perspectives demonstrate the continued need for marginalised feminisms to theorise gender analysis from the perspectives, world views and lived experiences of non-Western women. Mekgwe defines African feminism as a discourse that:

> Takes care to delineate those concerns that are peculiar to the African situation. It also questions features of traditional African cultures without denigrating them, understanding that these might be viewed differently by the different classes of women. (2003, 7)

African feminisms critique and reject dominant narratives that generalise and essentialise the condition of African women, men and children and seek awareness of specific contexts, cultures and peoples. Such an approach requires describing particular national or regional trends, while simultaneously raising awareness of contextual variations within broader trends. African feminisms in addition emphasise the power and agency of African women in particular to theorise from their cultures and lived experiences to produce knowledge that is contextually relevant, builds relationships, heals the self, the community and the larger socio-cultural context. Some African feminists, for instance, prefer the term womanism to feminism, arguing that the term feminism is associated with Western ideologies. From this womanism perspective arose the term Africana womanism to describe the particular experiences of people of African origin, both diasporic and indigenous. Africana womanism, for example, claims that the solutions to gender inequality should be found in African philosophy. Explaining the Africana womanism position Hudson-Weems notes,

> Essentially, the Africana womanism position is that the framework for a world free of oppression already exists within traditional African philosophical world view – if only the Africana woman will claim it. (in Yaa Asantewaa Reed 2001, 175)

The philosophical world view of the Bantu of Southern Africa is that a 'being' is essentially bound with others: 'I am we; I am because we are; we are because I am' (Goduka 2000). A person 'is' through others. This principle is in direct contrast to the Eurocentric view of humanity; 'I think, therefore, I am' (Descartes). The former expresses a concept of self that is individually defined and 'is in tune with a monolithic and one-dimensional construction of humanity' (Goduka 2000, 29). In the principle, 'I am because we are', 'the group has priority over the individual without crushing the individual, but allowing the individual to blossom as a person' (Senghor 1966, 5). *Existence-in-relation* and *being-for-self-and-others* sum up the African conception of life and reality (Oyewumi 1998, 398). Black feminists (Collins 2000; Johnson-Bailey 2006) share similar views about relational existence. For example, in writing about African American women's collective voice and experience, Collins states, 'the voice that I know is both individual and collective, personal and political reflecting the intersection of my unique biography within the larger meaning of my historical times' (2000, vi).

The African philosophical view promotes an ethical framework that emphasises the responsibilities of researcher as transformative healer, working with the community and actively involved in healing, building communities and promoting harmony. A common thread that cuts across African feminisms is the emphasis on healing methods as necessary research tools for life-enriching and transformative experiences as well as spiritual growth for girls/women suffering from multiple oppressions and domination (Dillard 2009). A reflective feminist researcher works with communities, listens with compassion and love to the girls/women stories and makes visible their stories and the healing methods that they employ when they communicate their life experiences. The question of how gender inequality manifests itself in the education system in Botswana and a framework arising from Batswana philosophical world views to address girls/women's oppressions is thus very important.

The third theme explores how non-Western feminists and post-colonial and indigenous feminists have used post-structural deconstruction methods to voice their discontent with the hegemonic intellectual apparatus. These feminists have reworked the underlying concepts of structure and agency to privilege both contextual and indigenous meanings. Patricia Hill Collins, writing about Black feminism, argues that knowledge is socially situated because it is based on experiences and different situations. This approach is upheld by African feminists who argue that oppressed groups can learn to identify their distinct opportunities to turn their condition of marginalisation into a source of critical insight about how the dominant society thinks and is constructed. If a standpoint is a place from which human beings view the world, we concur with Harding (2004) that all standpoints (Western and the marginalised non-Western) are partial and co-exist.

The last theme centres on how African and Asian feminist and other non-Western feminists aim to move gender research towards post-colonial and indigenous approaches and the construction of knowledge derived from the experiences of girls/women in their specific locations and histories. Non-Western feminisms call for the critique, decolonisation and indigenisation of the literature and theory about the 'other' and Euro-Western methodologies. They propose and describe methodologies of reading literature, employing theory and conducting research that resist all forms of patriarchal and imperial oppression (Dube 2000). They also urge scholars to find and highlight theory and theorising in spaces perhaps not deemed 'theoretical from a Western academic perspective' (Saavedra and Nymark 2008, 258); to employ theoretical frameworks that are eclectic and combine theories and techniques from disparate disciplines and paradigms to construct their own paradigms (Sandoval 2000) and to demonstrate 'what indigenous cultures can offer in terms of concrete ways to read/re-read our current situations in the world' (Dillard 2009, 278).

Marshall and Young (2006, 65) argues that we must view gender research as a revolution and that methodology used to investigate gender issues must involve 'assertive question shifting, redefinition of issues, sharp attention to the power of dominant values, and vigilant monitoring to how questions are asked and how research is used'. Chilisa (forthcoming) suggests that when we read the literature and conduct research in formerly colonised countries such as those in the developing world, we need to ask ourselves the following questions:

- Does Western and imperialising literature, theory and research methods expose and show non-Western women's resistance to the multiple patriarchal systems that oppress women and what do alternative theories, literatures and research methodologies offer?
- Does the research demonstrate a genuine search for alternative research methodologies that respects indigenous relational worlds and promotes interdependence between world views, knowledge systems, nations, races, ethnicities, gender and sexual orientations and with what alternative research methodologies does it achieve this objective?
- How does this research employ indigenous knowledge and literature to reject empire and envision alternative methodologies that rename the experiences of non-Western women from their standpoints, and envisions other ways of representing voices of women and other oppressed groups in research reports?
- Is the research 'action-oriented' and 'values-oriented'?

We use these questions as a framework to highlight how Western liberal feminist theory has become dominant and promotes state-led top-down policy initiatives as the primary means of addressing gender inequalities. How do we as feminist researchers for instance, address what Unterhalter (2006) calls 'issues of methodology and the power entailed in the "colonial gaze", the process by which research participants become "gendered" ... and the silencing and erasure of women from many conventional sources of data collection'? We illustrate methodological imperialism by questioning the universal application of confidentiality and anonymity in social science research and argue that in some contexts in the developing world these codes at times protect the individual at the expense of disempowered groups or even the community in general (Chilisa 2005). These research practices in our view are testimony to how the universal application of Euro-Western methods can conceal the oppression of marginalised and oppressed groups such as girls/women. Elabor-Idemudia, expressing a concern about the universal application of Euro-Western methods asks,

> How is it possible to decolonise (social) research in/on the non-Western developing countries to ensure that the people's human condition is not constructed through Western hegemony and ideology? (2002, 231)

What do we as researchers, for instance, do when research participants express their world views in metaphorical language, in praise song, folklore, myth or in symbolic cultural artifacts? Chambers (1994) recommends that indigenous practices and beliefs be noted, and even if they do not fit in with conventional scientific thinking (e.g. practices based on myth or superstition). In an effort to decolonise dominant methodologies it is becoming necessary to analyse local folklore, songs, dance, and poetry to provide insight into the values, history, practices, and beliefs of formerly colonised societies. In support of this view, Elabor-Idemudia notes:

> Oral forms of knowledge, such as ritualistic chants, riddles, songs, folktales, and parables not only articulate, a distinct cultural identity but also give voice to a range of cultural, social and political, aesthetic, and linguistic systems – long muted by centuries of colonialism and cultural imperialism. (2002, 100)

Part of being a feminist activist in a developing world we argue is to recognise sayings, proverbs, rituals and songs from our research respondents as part of the missing literature that has been muted by Euro-Western methodologies largely dominated by male thought. This indigenous knowledge makes visible the spaces of agency ever so present in the life experiences of marginalised feminisms and yet so absent in the academic debate. Listening to the sayings, observing the rituals we argue, makes visible the culture-based ideologies of oppression and how women are resisting the gender order that comes with cultural ideologies as well as reveal women's resistance to conventional research methods in preference for other methods that resonate with their world views. We argue that through these methods contextual-based concepts and frameworks that communicate the experiences of girls/women can become visible to the academic debate on gender inequalities. We also foreground indigenous, African feminisms as a framework to understand and interpret gender, regulation, resistance and activism in education and research. We will begin with an overview of how educational policies, informed by feminist liberal theory in the guise of redressing gender inequalities, reaffirm male power.

Liberal feminism and gender equality policies in Botswana education policy

Liberal feminist theory has strongly influenced 'Women in Development' (WID) policies that have dominated educational policy in Botswana. Liberal feminisms focus on the subordination of women through unequal opportunities that are institutionalised through the legal, political, social and economic structures. The various versions of liberal feminism insist that women's opportunities should be equal with men's and that policies, legislations and statutes should be put in place to address social injustices between the sexes. It is in the context of this liberal feminist framework that Botswana in 1996 put in place the policy on WID which outlined measures and programmes designed to address, among others, inequalities in the education and training of girls/women. One of the main concerns was that although there were more girls enrolled at primary and junior secondary school, female enrollment decreased at senior secondary school and tertiary institutions. The reasons for these disparities of access were that boys outperformed girls in national examinations that formed the basis for selection for advancement to upper levels of education and that many girls dropped out of school due to pregnancy. There was also a concern that girl/women enrollment in vocational and technical institutions never exceeded 35%. Factors contributing to low enrollment in vocational training and science-related subjects were listed as: (1) gender-biased teaching materials; and (2) gender-biased stereotyping during the socialisation in the family, at school and in the communities in general.

Despite policy efforts based on the WID framework, in 2003, Botswana needed a gender equality in education index (GEEI) of 21.79% to reach the adequate GEEI index of 95% (Unterhalter 2006). Critics argue that research informed by the WID framework has failed to adequately address gender inequalities because it interprets equality generally in terms of equal numbers of human and physical resources or equal number of images in textbooks but fails to address the complex gender equality and inequalities in schools, the diversity of experiences of girls and their negotiations and resistance to oppression (Fennell and Arnot 2009; Unterhalter 2006). Despite these shortcomings, research informed by the WID framework continues to shape international gender and education agendas that import liberal individualising models of education and undermine girls/women positions thus aggravating existing gender divisions (Fennell and Arnot 2009; Unterhalter 2006). This is mainly because gender education research is funded by international agencies from the developed world which encourage a one-way traffic of universal gender theory that follows from Northern America and Europe to the South. The current trend by African and Asian feminist and other nonWestern feminists to move gender research towards postcolonial and indigenous approaches propels feminist researchers to revisit gender research and to ask which and whose research is used.

The WID policy was followed by the Gender and Development (GAD) policy. GAD set out as one of its main strategies to mainstream gender into all sections of education to achieve equity in educational access and retention; enhance the quality of the life of students and teachers; enable equal participation of male and female students across subjects and choice of careers; ensure equal participation of female and male teachers in the teaching of all subjects and to implement schooling sexualities that equally empower girls and boys. In addition, Botswana acceded to the Convention on the Rights of the Child (CRC) in 1995, the Convention on the Elimination of All Forms of Discrimination Against Women in 1996 and signed the African Charter on the Rights and Welfare of the Child (ACRWC) in July 2001. Vision 2016, a long-term plan aimed at improving the lives of Batswana in general and promoting the quality of life of the girl child in particular, informs policy planning and practice in Botswana. The emphasis of vision 2016 is 'gaining empowerment by empowering others', an ideal that resonates with the GAD policy.

In an effort to address gender violence, statutes on the school-age group have been reviewed to protect the girls against defilement, sexual harassment, early marriages and pregnancies (Ministry of Labor and Home Affairs 1998). Defilement defined as sexual intercourse with any girl below the age of 16 carries a maximum of life imprisonment. In practice, however, many men do not serve the full term. For instance, In the Keraetse 1995 court case (Alexanda et al. 2005), a man accused of defilement of a girl between the age of 14 and 15 years had his sentence reduced from five years to three years and then was given a two years suspended sentence on the basis that the man could not be expected to ask the girl to produce a birth certificate in a situation where a girl past puberty invites sexual relations. In the Kgathileng 1993 case (Alexanda et al. 2005), a school teacher convicted of defilement of a 13-year-old pupil had his sentence changed to indecent assault and was sentenced to one year and two months on the argument that there was no vaginal penetration. The implementation of the policies is compromised by contradictory messages sent through tradition, customary law, legislation and policies on the definition of a girl child. The Children's Act (1981), currently under review, defines a child as any person under the age of 18 years while the Disserted Wife's and Children's Protection defines a child as any person below the age of 16 years. The Children in Need of Care Regulations (2005), on the other hand, defines a child as any person under the age of 14 years. Events or development features are also invoked to mark childhood and adulthood. The girl child would mean a young girl and in Setswana this may mean the period before a person has received their first menstrual period, 'go rupa' in Setswana. Marriage is also used as a yard stick to differentiate between a girl child and a woman. Under customary law, the legal age of marriage remains unclear as no age is stipulated. Among some ethnic groups in the country, under customary practice, for instance, a 14-, 15- or 16- year-old girl may get married to an older man (Alexander et al. 2005). These differences in interpretation of a child expose girls to gender violence. It would appear in the Keraetse (1995) court case, for instance, that the judges invoked cultural practice among some ethnic groups that puberty marks a girls entry into womanhood, thus a 14-year-old who has reached puberty would not be protected by the statute. This appears to apply a Western liberal representation of women as 'other' and 'victim' in the developing world that demonises and homogenises indigenous cultures and also assumes that there is no gender justice in these cultures and definitely offered no opportunity to seek out challenges to gender violence in the local cultural practices. We need to ask also, do girl children suffer oppression from the seemingly protective universalised Western liberal thought and its administration of justice that privileges the male voice? How is gender research conducted and used and how is indigenous literature employed to inform empowerment strategies?

Children's voices and research methods

Marshall and Young note that

> Research alone, no matter what the methodology, cannot prevent backsliding or fix gender and education challenges unless it is action- and values-oriented, as it challenges hegemony with world-changing findings. (2006, 72)

Our research explored children's voices on experiences of gender violence in Botswana Primary and Junior Secondary schools to question the use of research, the ethics involved, and the roles and responsibilities of a feminist activist researcher and to reveal the spaces of agency informed by indigenous relational worlds that girls create. Until recently, in conventional research, children were not consulted but spoken for by others (Leach 2006). New research is illustrating the international contexts in which children's voices are foregrounded in research on gendered violence in schools (Leach and Mitchell 2006). We illustrate gender violence through the study, *Telling Their Stories* (UNICEF 2005). The purpose of the project was to record the voices of children between the ages of 10 and 19 attending Primary and Secondary schools. Story telling was the main method for documenting the children's voices. In total 10,771 children were interviewed and 40 stories were collected. The stories and voices from the children show that there is violence in the school. This violence takes the form of sexual harassment by some teachers and community members, verbal abuse in the school and in the home, and physical abuse. The story below from a 14-year-old in a Primary school illustrates sexual harassment by a school head.

> We were in class writing our English compositions and submitted them to the school head. After he completed marking them our books were returned to us, with the corrections that were to be made. My friend and I were then told to go to the office. All of a sudden he decided that he did not want my friend there because her work was fine so she went back to class. After my friend left he told me that he wanted to talk to me and proceeded to tell me to go and fetch my books and school bag. So I went and fetched my bag and books. Upon arrival he wasted no time in caressing my breasts and private area. He then told me not to tell anyone.
>
> When I got home I reported my incident to my uncle and he told me that he would go to school and handle the matter. The following day he gave us another composition. To my surprise I was given 1/20, marks that I had not expected at all and again I was summoned to the office. When I got there he held my hand and said,
>
> 'O timana dijo, ga nke o tla kwa go nna' (You refuse with food, you never come to see me don't you want me?) I told him that I did not want him and he replied 'letsatsi leno o tsile go lala o mpatlile' (Today you will see me).
>
> He then proceeded to tell me that he knows my family and it did not matter. If he wanted he could even drop me off at home with his car and there would be no problem. Another teacher came by and he pretended as if he was helping me with my work. He then whispered to me that he would drop me at home.
>
> I have on several times told my uncle since the incident. At first he said he would go and see him but now all he says is that I am troubling him with women's issues. I then decided to tell mom and she is yet to come if she does at all. I really cannot concentrate in class and do not perform to the best of my ability, as a result I end up writing nonsense. (UNICEF 2005)

Three similar stories were collected from the same school. What is our role as feminist activist researchers when we come across such stories? In the case above, the sponsor of the research project wanted to take up the issue with the Ministry of Education. However, there were problems arising from the universal application of confidentiality and anonymity in social science research. The researchers promised anonymity and confidentiality on all data gathered through the project. The name of the schools, the teachers, school heads and the children thus remained anonymous and each participant was promised confidentiality. Worse still, there were no ethical guidelines on what to do in the event that the researcher discovered that some children were at risk. The universal application of confidentiality and anonymity in social science research was upheld. The perpetrator of violence remained nameless, without a face and untouched, while the oppression of the girls remained the same.

Elsewhere Chilisa (2011) notes that researchers in the formerly colonised societies in the developing world have a choice on what identity and ethical stance to adopt. They can operate at the level of coloniser co-opted by the dominant Western discourse on methodology, that uses Euro-Western standards as universal truths against which the 'other' former colonised societies marginalised by globalisation is researched and written about. At another level they can operate as healers, challenging and resisting the dominant Euro-Western application of methodologies across all cultures. At this level they see themselves as either members of the formerly colonised, marginalised and oppressed or as sympathisers, working with the communities to take action against oppression. These positions require knowledge production approaches that are multiple, interconnected, sensitive and engaging the researcher with ethical issues that position the researcher as healer where the healer engages with community to assist others to heal and to build harmony and bring about social transformation. In many ways this approach resonates with feminist action research models (Marshall and Young 2006) at work in Western contexts, but brings in the explicit dimension of postcolonial understandings of implementing Western research technologies. The researcher needs to ask the following questions:

(1) What is my purpose as a researcher?
(2) Do I challenge and resist dominant discourses that marginalise those who suffer oppression?
(3) What needs to be done to bring about social transformation and heal those who are suffering?

Although in the research described above, the researchers were not able to take any action, in research on gender violence in Ghana, Leach (2006) reveals how the researchers worked with the district education authorities and the community to expose a case of serious sexual misconduct. It was revealed that a community event called *durbar* was called where several thousands of people including local elders and district officials attended. During the *durbar* pupils performed a play written by the researcher on a head teacher asking girls for sexual favours. Following the *durbar*, an investigation was launched which confirmed the children's stories. The research illustrates the role of an activist feminist researcher as a transformative healer, resisting dominant research discourses that refuse to name oppression and engineering a process of healing in the community that comes with the knowledge that justice has been done. We look inside the classroom to further reveal gender oppression of girls and their negotiation and resistance power.

Inside the classroom: the gender order and triple oppression

Separateness, border lines, gender marked spaces, masculinised and feminised subjects also characterise almost all the schools in Botswana (Chilisa 2005; Dunne et al. 2005). This gender order is very often rehashed through traditional ideologies marketed thorough vernacular language, such as proverbs and sayings in a hybrid mix with Western religion taught in subjects like Moral Studies and Religious Knowledge. In almost all the classes in Botswana schools, the seating patterns reveal stark gender division of space with boys physically distanced from girls (Chilisa et al. 2005; Dunne 2008; Dunne et al. 2005). At school assemblies and in queues for food, boys and girls line up separately. The teachers seem to treat separation of girls' and boys' spaces as common-sense practice. Some teachers invoke their own cultural beliefs that naturalise the boundary between men and women to justify these seating patterns in classrooms. Some teachers invoke the Setswana culture belief that *men who associate with women are supposed to be weaklings* (*ke bo pheramesesing*). They further couple Setswana culture with religion to justify the gender order. One teacher observed as follows:

> A man is of a higher status than a woman. A woman is of the status of a child. Also, a woman is made from a man's rib that's maybe the reason why girls/women would prefer to be closer to boys/men.

Men's attempt to fashion an identity separate from women is not new. Western feminists trace the origin to Plato's theory of mind/body split. According to Plato we all have an immortal soul that knows all. However, what is known is forgotten at birth when our soul inhabits our bodies. According to Plato our bodies cause us to forget, compelling us to spend our lifetime trying to remember what we knew before birth. The argument is that in the Euro-Western philosophy, girl/woman is excluded from the concept of 'human being' through the association of man with mind and therefore reason and rationality and girl/woman with body and irrationality (Thayer-Bacon 2003). The mind/body split, rational/irrational, reason/emotion split cast girl/woman as 'other' defined in relation to boy/man and marginalised and peripheral. Women are cast on the side of body because of their reproductive role and because they menstruate, a condition associated with mood swings and emotional drama. Some male teachers, for instance, even suggested that the clustering of the boys in class was caused by girls' menstrual periods. It was reported (by the teachers) that girls sometimes had their menstruation in class and occasionally would mess up chairs. Boys shunned the girls for this. So they tended to keep a 'safe' distance away from them. During menstruation among some ethnic groups, the girls miss classes. Once they are pregnant, the expectation is that they must stop attending classes with the rest of the learners. When they do they are subjected to ridicule, harassment and isolation by other learners who believe that they make them sleepy (Chilisa 2002). The male teachers' resistance to encourage equality of boys and girls is thus simply an extension of global male stream hegemony constructed along binary opposites of the rational man and the irrational woman reduced to a low social status through the assignment of a sexual body. What comes out clearly is that both boys and teachers invoke both local culture and Western religion to justify the gender order in the school. This illustrates how gender oppression drawn from the hybrid context works together to create gender oppressions, and illustrate the need to challenge oppressive norms coming from each of these roots. This is clearly evident again in data from the following study on gender, sexuality, HIV/AIDS and life skills education (Chilisa et al. 2005, see also Morrell et al. 2009), where for instance, a gender order that placed boys first in their social hierarchy emerged from interviews with moral and education teachers. In some of the interviews the gender order emerged as follows:

> Interview: Is there any difference between what boys and girls say concerning HIV/AIDS and life skills topics?

Teacher:	Mostly, they disagree on topics that concern females and males, for example we had a topic that was on morality and religion, and then asked them about the fact that all religious leaders are males. I was enquiring from them whether that shows a fact of fairness or inequality. The boys said that the females should be at home. The reason being that if God wanted females to be leaders, He could have made the first woman to be a leader. The first person was a man Adam. The woman was made from the rib of Adam. Even Jesus was a male. So, we ought to follow the trend. The girls are saying we can change from that. Again, the people who wrote the Bible are males, so they would portray Jesus as male and not female.
Interviewer:	This idea of male leadership, where do you think it came from?
Teacher:	I feel it comes from home. They even mentioned the Setswana proverb, 'ga dinke di etelellwa ke manamagadi pele' (Men are born leaders, women are followers) … Again they argue that the reason why women cannot lead is because they like bragging and are short-tempered and easily tempted. They gave an example of Eve, who was the first to be tempted and influenced by the devil. They also gave an example of Delilah who tempted Samson. The girls would at the same time disagree. One of them said she was hurt by what the boys were saying and said that women were meant to help men make decisions and not men to make decisions.

The highlighted sections show how patriarchal views congealed from Christian and Setswana knowledge bases.

In another ongoing study (Chilisa 2009), boys and girls were asked questions on who makes decisions on boyfriend and girlfriend relationships. Some of the respondents invoked the same proverb to argue that a boy should make decisions all the time. In an effort to determine the frequency of this belief, 107 students were asked to respond to a question in which one of the items required them to strongly agree, agree, disagree or strongly disagree with the proverb. The responses were further collapsed into two columns with strongly agree to agree forming an 'agree' code and agree to strongly disagree forming a 'disagree'. The majority of the boys agreed with the proverb while almost all the girls disagreed.

How does an activist feminist researcher address oppression that comes through religion, and local, African cultural ideologies and the patriarchal privileging of the male voice? African feminism asserts that 'the framework for a world free of oppression already exists within traditional African philosophical world view', which can be used to challenge the patriarchal myths in African cultures. We want to ask what narratives the African philosophical world view offers to counter proverbs like: 'Ga dinke di etelelwa ke e namagadi pele, di ka wela ka le mina' (Women cannot be leaders) and the Western Biblical story of human origin?

The Tswana story of origin offers one alternative (are there more?). According to the Tswana story of origin, the people came from the hill of Lowe. When they came out, men and women were walking side-by-side driving sheep, goats and cattle. This story defies explanations that justify inequalities on the basis of traditions and reveals other ways of viewing gender relations based on tradition. It is an important contribution to knowledge production in the area of gender relations and could be used as an important entry point for a researcher who might be looking for intervention strategies to address the inequalities. We can see how there are important resources in African philosophy to challenge gender oppressions and we need to ask questions about how this can be used methodologically and educationally to challenge gendered violence, for instance.

Listening to voices of resistance and promoting healing methods

There is no doubt that participatory methods that promote social justice and heal girls/women from patriarchal oppressions by religion, culture and their men are essential to the fight against gender oppression. The challenge is to listen to the girls'/women's voices and the indigenous cultures that inform culture-based oppression as well as document the indigenous cultures that name girls/women differently and the indigenous research methods that resonate with women's experiences. Songs are, for instance, used as a feminist research method that reveal cultural ideologies that oppress girls/women, but they can also reveal women's resistance to patriarchy and as a healing strategy for those who suffer oppression, although we have not explored enough the research instances where this is happening. Songs and dance allow women to relive their experiences and to get in their worlds and express their innermost feelings. Singing together also allows them to collectively share the pain of patriarchal oppression and to heal through the knowledge that they collectively resist the dominance. Listening to songs that women sing in research with women is a method that approaches the researched in a comfortable and non-threatening manner, and also allows the researcher to start from the researched point of reference.

In a case study on female leadership and empowerment in Botswana, Ntseane (2009) describes how the women research participants resisted the use of conventional interview method and insisted on the use of songs and utensils to communicate their life experiences. She notes that instead of using the interview guide that the researcher had prepared for data collection, some groups of women requested that the researcher listen to songs about their leader's attributes; stories about the leadership nicknames of female leaders/leadership and traditional words that adequately describes the power of female leadership. A group of women belonging to an opposition political party for example, suggested that they sing a song. This song narrated the story of their female leader and also gave them an opportunity to demonstrate via song her power and authority by acting out how she embodies respect in her dealings with other politicians. The rich and detailed description embedded in the song included this translated quotation: 'when our capable one walks to council for a meeting, you can't miss her humbled confidence and preparedness as demonstrated by her non-verbal communication actions'. The women also insisted on other ways of conducting focus group interviews not common in the literature. The excerpts below illustrate the execution of the methods.

Focus Group and the Use of a Magic Wooden Spoon

> In one of the focus group discussions, the women insisted that they use a wooden spoon to guide the discussions instead of a focus group moderator. The focus group started with one of the women saying: '*to ensure that we all contribute let us use this magic stick to help process our thoughts and contribute when it is appropriate*'. The researcher was also requested to be part of the focus group because as one put it, '*as a woman like us you also have to share the wisdom that you have. The spoon says you have to eat something (no matter how small) from the same pot with us but also put in something even if it is just one fire wood or a drop of water. Everyone is capable of doing something, thus the spoon has to go round and not skip anybody*'. The use of a spoon symbolises collective decision-making (i.e. the idea that no one person can know it all, but several scoops of wisdom from other members help shape and refine an idea to make it a useful decision).

The Use of a Basket

In another focus group, a woman suggested that the host put a basket in the middle of the focus group. Asked what the role of the basket was, this is how one of the women responded: '*When women commit to coming together it is because they want to collect something that will contribute to the welfare of their children or community. We see your study as giving you, us and the other women in the other three countries participating in the study to contribute to a bigger purpose*'. The basket represents a 'vision or goal' thus to successfully implement the goal, each individual's contribution and participation is required. Having the basket in the middle of the focus group is a reminder and motivation for contribution. In fact, this is how one respondent kept using the basket to encourage the group to think hard about what the issues, '*this basket is half full, or is almost full. We can't take it to other women in Africa not full. What will they think of us and our society?*'

Compared to the use of conventional Western-based and scientifically organised research methods and techniques, the use of context-specific and indigenous methodologies still have to be documented as part of exploring and developing research methodologies. The methods also invite us to reflect on the research techniques we are using in developing contexts we use in the education system to research gender oppression of the girl child. They invite us to move to healing research methods that allow research participants to name and share pain and to collectively envision strategies for resistance, resilience and survival. There is much research experience from this arena to contribute to debates in novel, participatory research methods, action research and feminist research internationally (Fennell and Arnot 2009; Marshall and Young 2006; Nnameka 1997). For instance, in representing the African context, rendering invisible and sometimes denying women's role as mothers, sisters or daughters, and inability to register small acts of resistance that achieve levels of empowerment has been an unfortunate outcome of colonially rooted research accounts (Fennell and Arnot 2009).

Participants in leadership study also requested feedback in the form of dissemination of the study findings in a way that would be useful and meaningful to their people. One participant noted:

> we have learnt a lot from participating in this study but because of the need to continue learning by sharing what we have learnt with other female leaders in the district the country and even internationally we want the results to be disseminated at our big Kgotla (public parliament) where other members of our ethnic group can confirm and expand on what we gave in the report.

Yet another said, 'female leaders from other districts as well as policy members should be invited' (dilo makwati di kwatabolotswa mo go ba bangwe) meaning brilliant ideas are generated from interactions with other people.

The idea of public and collective feedback in the local language was perceived as essential for continued development of female leadership strategy in this context. It is clear that this type of feedback resists the current conventional research feedback of journal articles to the educated elites and research reports to government policy decision makers and donors which use a language foreign to the source of the information. Given the demand for public feedback to the source of research knowledge, the implications for the role of the researcher is that he/she should be an activist and for research to be reciprocal. One respondent noted:

> We are tired of researchers who come here; get our knowledge, experiences and problems only to give to people we don't know. This time we want our own people in the

South East District as well as other Batswana who want to know what we do as female leaders in our part of the country to be invited to the public (Kgotla) dissemination. Then we will feel that our participation in this study had an impact and not a waste of time.

The quote takes us back to the voices from children on gender violence in the school and provokes researchers to think about ways in which we can decolonise research so that it benefits the researched. The women's resistance to the conventional focus group techniques in preference for indigenous approaches is a wakeup call to those who still think other cultures/groups/gender ways of research can continue to be marginalised. We take it that this means that researchers have to be activists as they have to use their research experiences to make a difference in the lives of those researched. In the leadership case study, it is clear that participants were co-researchers because their indigenous methods were found to be the most appropriate in that cultural research context.

Conclusion

In this paper we have explored the ways in which male hegemony is reinforced through Western religion as well as traditional African male-biased constructions of girls/women, embedded in Tswana language and rituals, generating multiple forms of oppression. We have also suggested, however, that some Western liberal informed policies that address gender inequalities and male-dominated Euro-Western methodologies provide little space for addressing the complexities of this male hegemony. We argue we need to develop new strategies for bringing social justice and healing into research that can account for girls' and women's resistances. We have demonstrated girls'/women's resistance to oppression, showing how they are creating local standpoints that promote sharing and working together against gendered oppressions and violences. We also illustrated how women are resisting conventional research methods in preference to socially just methods, in line with other research on feminist action and participatory research (Collins 2000; Johnson-Bailey 2006; Nnameka 1997) that promote listening with respect, love, thinking together and healing. We have also argued that indigenous knowledge rooted in relational world views promotes the thinking and working together and interdependence between men and women that is necessary to address gender inequalities. Decolonising research processes in turn helps envision other ways of theorising the complexity of gender and educational experiences. It is this understanding that will help to build bridges to enable the formation of genuine alliances between indigenous and Western feminisms that are grounded in ethicality and transformative respect and healing.

References

Alexander, E., G. Lesetedi, L. Pilane, E. Mukaamambo, and R. Masilo-Rakgaasi. 2005. *Beyond inequalities: Women in Botswana*. Gaborone: WIDSAA.

Ashcroft, B., G. Griffiths, and H. Tiffin. 1991. *The Empire writes back*. London: Routledge.

Chambers, R. 1994. Participatory Rural Appraisal (PRA): Challenges potentials and paradigm. *World Development* 22: 1437–54.

Chilisa, B. 2002. National policies on pregnancy in the education system in Sub-Saharan Africa: A case of Botswana. *Gender and Education Journal* 14, no. 1: 21–35.

Chilisa, B. 2005. Educational research within postcolonial Africa: A critique of HIV/AIDS research in Botswana. *International Journal of Qualitative Studies* 18: 659–84.

Chilisa, B. 2009. Indigenous African-centred ethics: Contesting complementing dominant models. In *The handbook of social research ethics,* ed. D. Mertens and P. Ginsberg, 407–25. Thousand Oaks, CA: Sage.

Chilisa, B. 2011. *Indigenous research methodologies.* Thousand Oaks, CA: Sage.
Chilisa, B., M. Dube-Shomanah, N. Tsheko, and Mazile Bontshetse. 2005. *The voices and identities of Botswana school children gender HIV/AIDS and life skills in education.* Gaborone: UNICEF Nairobi.
Collins, P.H. 2000. *Black feminist thought: Knowledge consciousness and politics of empowerment.* 2nd ed. New York: Routledge.
Dillard, C.M. 2009. When the ground is black, the ground is fertile: exploring endarkened feminist epistemology and healing methodologies of the spirit. In *Handbook of critical and indigenous methodologies*, eds. M. Denzin, Y. Lincoln and L. Smith, 227–291. Thousand Oaks, CA: Sage.
Dube, M. 2000. *Postcolonial feminist interpretation of the bible.* St Louis, MO: Charles Press.
Dunne, M. 2008. *Gender sexuality and development: Education and society in sub-Saharan Africa.* Rotterdam: Sense Publishers.
Dunne, M., and F. Leach, with B. Chilisa, R. Tabulawa, and T. Maundeni. 2005. *Gendered school experiences: Impact on retention and achievement, in Botswana and Ghana.* London: DFID.
Elabor-Idemudia, P. The retention of knowledge of folkways as a basis for resistance. In *Indigenous knowledge in global contexts*, eds. G. Dei, B. Hall and D. Rosenberg, 102–119.
Fennell, S., and M. Arnot. 2009. Decentralizing hegemonic gender theory: the implications for educational research. RECOUP Working Paper no. 21, Development Studies and Faculty of Education, University of Cambridge.
Goduka, I. N. 2000. African or indigenous philosophies; legitimizing spiritually centered wisdoms within the academy. In *African voices in education*, eds. P. Higgs, N. C. G. Vakalisa, T. V. Mda and N. T. Assie-Lumumba, 63–83. Lansdowne: Juta.
Harding, S. 2004. *Introduction: Standpoint theory as a site of political philosophical and scientific debate.* New York: Routledge.
Johnson-Barley, J. and Alfred, M. V. 2006. Transformational teaching and the practices of Black Women adult educators. *New Directions for Adult and Continuing Education,* 109: 49–58. Published online in Wiley InterScience (www.wiley.com) DOI:10.1002/ace.207.
Leach, F. 2006. Researching gender violence in schools: Methodological and ethical considerations.World Development 34, no. 6: 1129–1147.
Leach, F., and C. Mitchell, eds, 2006. *Combating gender violence in and around schools*, Stoke on Trent, UK: Trentham Books.
Marshall, C., and M. Young. 2006. Gender and methodology. In *The Sage handbook of gender and education,* ed. C. Skelton, B. Francis, and L. Smulyan, 63–78. London: Sage.
Mekgwe, P. 2003. Theorizing African feminisms: The colonial question. Paper presented at the Department of English Seminar Series, University of Botswana, in Gaborone.
Ministry of Labor and Home Affairs. 1998. Botswana Government, Gaborone Printers.
Mohanty, C. 1991. Under western eyes: Feminist scholarship and colonial discourses. In *Third world women and the politics of feminism,* ed. C. Mohanty, A. Russo, and L. Torres, 51–80. Bloomington: Indiana University Press.
Morrell, R., D. Epstein, E. Unterhalter, and D. Bhana. 2009. *Towards gender equality: South African schools during the HIV and AIDS epidemic.* KwaZulu-Natal: University of KwaZulu-Natal Press.
Nnameka, O., ed. 1997. *The politics of mothering: Womanhood, identity and resistance in African literature.* London: Routledge.
Ntseane, P.G. 2009. *Community leadership and empowerment: Botswana case study.* Kampala: Institute of Social Transformation.
Oyewumi, O. 1998. DeConfounding gender: feminist theorizing and western culture. *Signs: Journal of Women in Culture and Society* 23, no. 4: 1049–1062.
Saavedra, C.M., and Ellen D. Nymark. 2008. Borderland and Mestiszaje feminism: The new tribalism. In *Handbook of critical and Indigenous methodologies,* ed. M. Denzin, Y. Lincoln, and L. Smith, 277–291. Thousand Oaks, CA: Sage.
Sandoval. C. 2000. *Methodology of the oppressed.* Minneapolis: University of Minnesota Press.
Senghor, L. 1966. Negritude. *Optima* 16: 1–8.
Thayer-Bacon, B. 2003. *Relational epistemologies.* New York: Peter Lang.
UNICEF. 2005. *Telling their stories.* Gaborone: UNICEF.

Unterhalter E. 2006. Education and Development. In *The Sage handbook of Gender and Education,* eds. C. Skelton B. Francis and L. Smulyan. 93–108. Thousand Oaks: Sage.

Yaa Asantewaa Reed, P.Y. 2001. African womanism and African feminism: A philosophical, literacy, and cosmological dialect on family? *Western Journal of Black Studies* 25: 168–76.

On the madness of lecturing on gender: a psychoanalytic discussion

Deborah P. Britzman

Faculty of Education, York University, Toronto, Canada

This essay comments on the emotional difficulties psychoanalytic discussion introduces to conceptualising the poesis of gender through its reconsideration of the valence of aggression and its development in psychical reality. It returns to the 1936 lectures on the emotional life of gender given by Melanie Klein and Joan Riviere to a public about to go to war. These psychoanalysts are known for representing 'the mad side' of gender and consider femininity and masculinity as lending emotional weight to the body and as one source for phantasy material that propels gender's reach into symbolisation, conflicts, and intersubjectivity. Their views are brought into tension with Winnicott's reconceptualisation of aggression in gender development. While historical questions on the relation between psychoanalytic theories of gender and the context of World War II are raised, Winnicott turns to a little war in the emotional life of gender to analyse traces of mental pain that its history leaves in its wake. He raises the new problem of the play between internal and external reality and how a one-sided take on gender as either masculine or feminine as the entire experience and goal of the body forecloses attempts to understand the self's gender work as both internal conflict and intersubjectivity. Loyalty to one side, or the defence of splitting into good and bad, itself the condition for war, has as one of its roots gender polarity. The madness of lecturing on gender resides in conveying this problem. My contribution leans on psychoanalytic allegory: that a return to historical discussion of psychoanalysis on the problems of representations of gender may allow reflection on our world of war and create elbow room needed to reconceptualise the currency, difficulties, and emotional obstacles repeated in contemporary pedagogical efforts and research.

Madness[1]

When lecturing on the topic of gender, words lent to the body take on uncanny abundance: there are fights about essentialist claims; gaps between experience and theory; discussions of 'gender trouble'; questions over the relations between nature and culture and between phantasy and reality; attempts to correct or defend stereotypical meanings through the splitting of gender into masculinity and femininity; discord over social and emotional meanings of terms such as gender, sex, sexuality, men, and women; and heated debate over the status and focus of social constructions, regulations, and resistance. There are hurt feelings and pedagogical failures. Additionally, when lecturing on how gender ought to be, the lecturer is apt to forget that ideas about gender are neither easily received nor viewed as a means for change, since gender involves an intimate resistance and an inchoate refusal to involve oneself in a circus of meanings. We may find that the lecture founders on the bedrock of biology or takes cover in the defence of conscious meanings. All this raises the questions of the emotional world of gender, the reach of its psychical representatives, and their tendencies of splitting.

Psychoanalysis proposes in mental life the additional factor of internal aggression, or bodily drives, as a needed element for the constitution of gender and that gives rise to phantasies of gender that complicate problems of its symbolisation. Psychoanalysts risk the soundings of a peculiar madness when trying to represent the internal world and the object relations that propose an impressive dispersal of the unconscious history of gender. They play in the field of the personal and the impersonal, feeling their way into gender as a combine of feelings in search of constructions. They also propose a constitutive gap between the given and received meanings of gender.

One of the first attempts to put such theories to the general public occurred in 1936, when the London Institute of Psychoanalysis sponsored two public lectures given by Melanie Klein and Joan Riviere, announced as 'The Emotional Life of Civilized Men and Women'. A year later they were published under the title 'Love, Hate, and Reparation', perhaps because the negativity of Riviere's opening topic, 'Hate, Greed, and Aggression', seemed to sound the death knell. Indeed, Riviere worried what the audience would take to heart and concluded on that note:

> An artificial segregation and discussion of the hate in emotional life, such as has been attempted here, is, you must remember, entirely schematic and is no representation of life as a whole. I hope that my presentation of it will not have proved depressing. It is of great importance that this side of our lives should be better understood. (1937, 52)

Then and now the delicate problem is whether, without having to take a side, we can begin to understand what *is* so one-sided, or rather so defended against and resisted, in attempts to represent the inside of gender. The danger is that this psychoanalytic orientation will propose and even act out both the madness of gender and the madness of trying to speak about it.

Riviere and Klein's lectures introduced to a general public about to go to war the concealments and displacements of aggression in emotional life. And they placed the evolution, dynamics, and phantasies of femininity and masculinity there. In doing so they proposed what is most startling about our gender madness and our endless struggles to feel its reasons. They also gave to aggression a precocious chronology that is best called 'phantasy', an inchoate constellation of helplessness, drives, anxieties, defences, and wishes that form the internal world of object relations and carry on through projections, introjections, and identifications. While there are a great many ways to think about aggression and gender within the psychoanalytic field, Klein and Riviere were the first to present the force of what is most inevitable about the gendered body – somatic trauma, psychical frustration, and constitutive anxiety – and what is most abstract and creative about our style of being: epistemophilia, or the drive to know, to represent, and to symbolise. Along with the entanglements of love and hate, they added one more dimension to aggression: it is ironic in its self-protective postulates and foolhardy in its destructive tendencies. Aggression, they argued, is needed to create the distinction between reality and phantasy and the difference within gender. For Klein and Riviere, there is something impossibly unreal about aggression: it originates interiority, ordains every one of its functions, defences, and wishes, and reverberates throughout gender and its transference.[2] There really isn't anything civilised in conveying and receiving a kernel of neurosis in any knowledge since trying to know plays with what is most uncivilised, or asocial, about emotional life: a tendency to collapse perception with the object.

The problem of symbolic equation, where internal affects collapse into an external object, is analysed in Jacqueline Rose's (1993) contemporary lectures on Melanie Klein and war. Rose considered violence and femininity, war in the nursery, and the death drive. She, too, brought what is most uncivilised to our attention and tried to respond to the anxiety that the magnification of phantasy and its negativity in emotional life might exclude, rather than deepen, awareness into the inexplicable and always terrible hostility found in the social world. There is, after all, a large problem with trying to discuss gender. It has to do with the fact that the body conveys 'being' without the consolation of knowing in advance how the other will receive it. Rose asked that we consider the problematic of this limit in our theories: 'what are the possible connections between an interrogation of problems of self-identification and sexuality in the unconscious and a field that can be called one of (conscious) knowledge and politics...?' (1993, 236). I add another dimension. It has to do with trying to represent phantasy, since identification and sexuality lend erotic force to its meanings. This leads to the question, where, when speculating on the experience of gender, can our madness play?

Here, then, are some ideas on gender madness, the madness involved in conveying gender to the other, the madness of gender itself, and the madness of lecturing on gender. My psychoanalytic approach experiments with matters of emotional life that unexpectedly bother, agonise, propose, and surprise our sense of gender as given, as unity, and as cohesion, all idealisations that seem to make gender feel so one-sided. I'll describe what Klein and Riviere make of gender and its aggression but will also press the limits of their understanding with Winnicott's approach to gender and aggression. Winnicott was analysed by Riviere and early in his psychoanalytic training was supervised by Klein (Winnicott 1996b). His views will lead to a new paradox of gender madness: we seem to find gender, destroy it, and then create it. These emotional activities are how Winnicott defines gender. In Winnicott's view, aggression in gender, however, feels as if it has been created before it can be found, and with this paradox a new understanding of destruction will emerge. Each of the three analysts – Klein, Riviere, and Winnicott – consider gender's madness differently, even as they maintain the innateness of bodily drives and consider aggressive drives as a constitutive force in emotional and social development. On these matters, we need not take sides since intra-psychic and inter-psychic processes are two sides of the same coin. In fact, one intimate dilemma of gender is that if we feel we may only have or occupy one side, we find and create the condition for war.

I turn to the idea of gender madness for three reasons, knowing full well we cannot give reasons to our reasons. First, I have been struck by the strangeness of trying to explain something like why we have gender at all, let alone what it means to attempt to affect its imaginary. And, given the transference, or the ways we unconsciously exchange authority, love, and knowledge, I have also felt that it is difficult to know when we are *not* talking about gender. This strangeness can be found in our classrooms, our theories, our activism, and in clinical practice. We can say with some certainty that one cannot be talked into gender or out of it even though gender seems to be an odd combination of given and received ideas, social pressure, and cosmetic manipulation. In fact, quite often, the idea of having or being a gender seems to be akin to meeting what the analyst Wilfred Bion called, 'thoughts that have no thinker' (1993, 165). Gender is there before consent, it is in the minds of those who come before us, and trying to think about gender brings us to what is most archaic in social and psychical life.

My second reason for focusing on gender madness emerges from a reconsideration of the admixture of feminism and its poststructural turn. We are used to the feminist ideal that the personal is political and now the poststructural one that both the political and the personal are historical and constructed and so resonate in the rubble of discourse. Along with taking the body through the linguistic turn we can add what Butler (1990) named, early on, 'gender trouble', or identity's performance anxiety. Yet, I am not sure we have sorted out just what the historical, the constructed, or the performative means let alone thought through the tension Pitt (2003) has called 'the play of the personal'. It may now be time to consider qualities of the personal that are deeply impressionable, impressive, and even excruciatingly impersonal and ahistorical. That is, there is something about gender that is also unconscious.

My third reason is really a hope that a notion of madness, sometimes also referred to as passion, may be a useful frame since gender is saturated with phantasies of one's own body, the body one does not have, and by the transitional space of creative play. The idea of madness conveys this entire scramble. This may seem like a long way from Klein and Rivere's lectures, or from Rose's needed question, but really, these thinkers teach us that there is always a conflict with the creation, transmission, reception, and unconscious meaning of both personal and political knowledge. The personal, all maintain, is also unconscious.

Now these ideas of the phantasy and symbolic space of gender play havoc with the political and every concept that must be taken for granted for something like the political to be postulated. When Rose (1993) attempts to hold the personal and political together, she does so by way of their destructive force, with the interminable question, 'Why war?' She brings to this clash the fact that there are three wars at stake: the inner world, the external world, and how the body lives the relation between these realities. Rose illustrates the conflict of these registers when she analyses the well-documented British Psychoanalytical Society's 1941–1945 Controversial Discussions between Melanie Klein and Anna Freud. This little war occurred between schools of thought and erupted in the midst of World War II. It concerned, among other things, whether psychoanalysis itself had to be one-sided and what happens to education in this collapse (Britzman 2003). The other controversy, still active today, concerns just how much the war imagery of psychoanalytic theory affects the psychoanalyst. Rose tells us that war is a terrible breakdown of knowledge and imagination, a foreclosure of the fact that as soon as knowledge becomes tied to the certainty of authority, both knowledge and imagination fail. But authority, as well, has a phantasy life that affects us all: in psychoanalysis it goes under the name of omnipotence, the drives, the super-ego, love and hate, the transference, guilt, and moral anxiety, and finds a home in our attitudes toward what is imagined as going right and wrong for gender.

In entering the personal – what we take too personally – Klein and Riviere's public lectures have some odd work to do. They take us beyond the brink of experience, reason, consciousness, and memory. They begin with what feels to be an unsolvable conflict between love and hate, show how it leads to guilt over destroying the object, and then insist that from this negativity comes the work of gratitude, love, and reparation, the elements for thinking, relationality, representation, and recognition of difference. At times, their claims lean upon the madness of absolutism yet still they manage to propose that knowledge of the emotional world can never be absolute since it may only begin when one can admit its vulnerability to loss, breakdown, frustration, and phantasy. Klein and Riviere suggest as well an unavoidable relation between feeling absolute certainty and defending against a primary helplessness. From all of this, they suppose, guilt and ambivalence allows knowledge of the world its transience, incompleteness, and fragility. There is an utter difficulty in learning from (as opposed to defending against) the travails of this emotional life.

Affect

Riviere thought of affects as both bodily passions and representations of the force of their history. She stayed with their negativity as her means for reaching into what is most disclaimed and disavowed about their vicissitudes and stunning outbursts. She also refused to separate affect from its roots in bodily distress. It is a counter-intuitive approach since in everyday parlance affect is considered as a product of consciousness. Riviere follows affect along its lines of the logic of psychical reality.

Riviere's (1937) lecture 'Hate, Greed, and Aggression', kept aggression close to love and hate, and linked it to our capacity to fight for what we believe is right. She argued that while hate is allied with destruction, love, too, has its destructive underside: we do not give up the libidinal object easily, the object is so easily lost, and thus love indicates a constitutive dependency on the object, a tie that is also hated. In proposing our right to love and so our fight against its vulnerabilities, Riviere insisted that aggression is never so far away. She kept close to the fact that our emotional life is emotional. Yet this leaves us with bare bones tautology: that emotions cause emotions. It is probably better to admit that we become entangled in the roots of our emotional life since, to say the least, the roots themselves are insecure because someone always waters them.

In a clinical essay on bereavement, written after the Second World War, Riviere argued that when we try to get at these emotional roots, we still meet contemporary entanglements:

> There is a tendency to experience events in later life in terms of earlier ones ... [and] we tend to explain unhappy events in personal terms; that is to say, we attribute them to some personal cause, essentially to some wrong-doing (as with the child to whom the loss of a pleasure means that his parents are punishing him). (1991a, 215)

These two emotional rules, all having to do with personal cause – or, what we take too personally – are the foundation of Klein and Rivere's lectures. There, the register of aggression oscillates between the sources, aims, and pressures of bodily drives and the Other's care needed to become a subject. In a very special sense, the madness and creativity of our emotional world lean upon this drive dilemma, and aggression is both the hallmark of this tiny war and, paradoxically, a destruction needed for symbolisation. This emotional world conveys our uneven development: our lifetimes are spent piecing together and fraying again the innumerable threads of what Klein, in her lecture 'Love, Guilt, and Reparation', simply called 'the emotional situation of the baby' (1937, 58).

The lectures are extraordinary in candour, in their passionate language, in their audacious sense of love and hate, and in the ways in which they magnify the already disproportionate unreason of bodily anxiety and defence, which they call phantasies. They insist that what is most difficult for the human is coming to terms with the fact of dependency, so linked as it is to the ensuing anxiety of losing the beloved object which will be equated with being left. For Riviere and Klein, the fact of dependency is a frustration that then incurs the hatred of dependency, itself a part of this fact. We can now get to their punch line: our original dependency on the mother will have an afterlife in how men and women imagine – through fears of persecution, punishment, envy, *and* with love, guilt, and reparation – the advent and vicissitudes of femininity and masculinity.[3]

Klein and Riviere tell an incredible story of the infancy of gender and sexuality as marked by a constitutive anxiety transferred through its surrogates: from the fact of dependency will come phantasies of destroying and being destroyed. Quite schematically, in Klein's (1975) view, humans begin their gender madness with the femininity phase, organised by their identification with and envy of the breast. Dependency on the mother saturates the child's phantasies of femininity, linking its meanings to fear of dependency, hostility toward this condition, and then desire to be separate. Separateness brings feelings of guilt and the awareness that the mother is a separate whole being. The infant loves and hates the same person. With the work of reparation a new meaning of separation and unity comes into being, and Klein proposed this work as the depressive position, an awareness of love's fragility and concern for the other.

Unlike melancholia, where nothing seems to matter at all, the depressive position is the beginning of poignant thinking, the capacity for guilt, and development of concern for the other. It is also the beginning of an awareness of the difference and relation between the internal and external world and a way to symbolise absence into something more than destitution and abandonment. Before all of that, as we will soon see, Klein posits the paranoid schizoid position, where the world is split into a terrible war between good and bad and attack and retaliation, a mad scramble that creates the need to project whatever feels bad in the self into others and then defend against the other's retaliation. This is what war feels like. There can be no real others since there is no meaning as to why the battle had to begin and since there is no meaning to the fact of dependency. In the psychological logic of emotions, dependency is just a bad thing to be defended against. Femininity may languish in this empty space and masculinity will imagine an escape. The tension is that Klein and Riviere locate this conflict within the body.

While Klein presents us with a bellicose tiny subject, it is not so apparent as to why the baby must be paranoid, or, why this war of love and hate? Indeed, in these lectures, the emotional situation of the baby reads like a miniature war theatre: from the beginning of life, the biting, kicking, crying, incontinent baby is always formulating and communicating its anxiety over absence and presence, equating absence with badness and presence with goodness. The baby is burning mad, particularly when she feels and must feel her utter dependency. The beginning is painful and devastating. In Riviere's words:

> If he feels emptiness and loneliness, an automatic reaction sets in, which may soon become uncontrollable and overwhelming, an aggressive rage which brings pain and explosive, burning, suffocating, choking bodily sensations; and these in turn cause further feelings of lack, pain and apprehension. The baby cannot distinguish between 'me' and 'not-me'; his own sensations are his world, *the* world to him; so when he is cold, hungry or lonely there is no milk, no well-being or pleasure in the world – the valuable things in life have vanished. And when he is tortured with desire or anger, with uncontrollable, suffocating screaming, and painful, burning evacuations, the whole of his world is one of suffering; it is scalded, torn, and racked too ... It is our first experience

of something like death, recognition of the non-existence of something, of an overwhelming loss, both in ourselves and others, as it seems. And this experience brings an *awareness of love* (in the form of desire), and *recognition of dependence* (in the form of need), at the same moment as, and inextricably bound up with, feelings and uncontrollable sensations of *pain and threatened destruction* within and without. (1937, 8–9)

No wonder Riviere worried about her audience's feelings. So did John Rickman (1937), whose preface to their book tries to warn readers what they are in for. The conflicts described will be felt and then, perhaps, disclaimed by this very reason. In one way, this was Riviere's worry: that magnifications of hate mean we are liable to lose all perspective. Our hope may take cover in depression. We may feel there is no way out. These lectures do empower infancy to such an extent that it never seems to go away. More so, they seem to be speaking for the baby who cannot yet speak, and the mother's voice is barely perceptible. Intellectual defences against their views also follow: neither Klein nor Riviere could prove that the baby has and projects phantasy into the other, that it made a story about its body and the other body without any knowledge at all, and that there was something already driven, already psychological about its mind. And, in a certain way, we cannot settle this account with any ease because, as Riviere worried, an account of our emotional world must be one-sided since so much depends upon what can never be remembered, since emotional life filters our perceptions of the object, and since the exploration of one's emotional world takes its lead from phantasy and play, all of which are experiences most adults hope to leave behind.

While Riviere worries about the audience's feelings, Rickman turns to a plea for feelings they may have but know nothing about. Rickman's advice and warning resides with the centrality of the unconscious in the lectures: remember, he writes, that the unconscious is antithetical to reason, to time, and to contradiction. Consciousness will be that struggle against its own unconscious representations. His advice concerns the ways Riviere and Klein move seamlessly between the child and the adult, as if no one can ever rid themselves of infantile despair, omnipotent thinking, and the talisman principle of an eye for an eye that governs the unconscious. Rickman writes:

> The fact is that the unconscious of the adult is actually not so very different from the mind of the child; it must be recognized, therefore, that in a certain sense psychoanalysts do attribute infantile thinking to grown-ups. (1937, vi)

Something about us does not grow up, and knowing this may return us to our oldest defences. And yet, his warning is really a plea for the reader's tolerance and open-mindedness, even as he concludes by understating a special difficulty that affects psychoanalysis as well: 'Not a little misunderstanding of psycho-analysis is due to a failure to realize that unconscious ways of thought and feeling are not only unconscious but are grasped only with difficulty' (Rickman 1937, v–vi).

Lest we begin to feel that psychoanalysis plunges us back into solipsism, or worse, the paranoid schizoid position, notice the ways in which the external world matters to what is being said. The psychoanalyst sees group psychology in each individual, although there are strong disagreements as to how the subject is thought to repeat, with great variation and without prior knowledge, their susceptibility to history, which includes the unconscious emotional history of parents, culture, and nation. In speaking about what the historical means in the psyche, André Green describes the historical as akin to a dream, a combination of what has happened, what has not happened, what could have happened, what has happened to someone else but not to me, what could not have happened ... [and] a statement that one would not have even dreamed of as a representation of what really happened. (2000a, 2–3)

The psychoanalyst is not immune from this dreamy history and indeed, through the transference, learns to lean upon her or his own inspired time (Britzman 2009). Unconscious life exhibits the odd paradox of being both formative and destructive, proposing the future of conflicts and serving as both their blind spot and their magnifying glass. So a large difficulty of learning the consequences of the historical, let alone trying to symbolise this, has to do with our capacity to play within the ever-shifting lines of the conscious and the unconscious, masculinity and femininity, and phantasy and reality.

Clinical knowledge

While Klein and Riviere's lectures give us a sweeping account of development, it is useful to consider how clinical knowledge constructs and conveys these difficult passionate matters. It must be said that its knowledge is not authoritative but vulnerable to the imagination and the unconscious play between the analytic couple. Paradoxically, clinical knowledge is not so far away from how infants acquire their sense of the world. Such knowledge takes as its starting point the force of phantasy, anxiety, and desire within the intersubjective sphere. Constructions made in the clinic are one way to symbolise the relation between the inner and external world, even as their language may return us to what is most disclaimed about both: namely the gendered afterlife of our fact of dependency. This fact weaves its way into rigid notions of masculinity and femininity that do find confirmation in the external world, but not without having to first pass through our own anxiety over loss of love.

In her discussion of Melanie Klein, Juliet Mitchell (1998) suggests the difficulty the clinician undergoes when trying to understand the other and how the clinician herself is changed. This is because clinical knowledge is made from

> being good at identifying with what one observes in order to follow what is going on in something other than oneself and then describing it [, which] constitutes an intermediary level of conceptualization ... Klein identifies and describes what intuitive identification and clinical observation are about: areas of confusion, fusion, lack of boundaries, of communicating without the differential structures of speech. (Mitchell 1998, 29)

Mitchell's depiction of Klein's technique of projective identification gives us a primary definition of gender as 'areas of confusion, fusion, lack of boundaries, [without] the differential structures of speech' (1998, 29). The psychic life of gender is an admixture of masculinity and femininity and so expresses the conflicts between them. Our private gender is also an on-going commentary on how we feel others feel about our bodies and pleasures. Projective identification is our permit into this madness. The danger is that in the act of trying to know, knowledge, too, carries a kernel of paranoia made from defences against the inconceivable.

The clinical relation lives within and creates this emotional tension and, as we will soon see, constructs a mad world where, paradoxically, one can feel sane because emotional actions may take place symbolically. The clinic can be considered as a container, not so much in terms of unifying gender or even aligning it with adaptation to reality, which would be an experience of compliance and actual aggression. Rather, the clinic provides a safe space where thinking can contain the play of the emotional life of gender and where phantasies of destruction can be sounded and symbolised. In this way the clinic contains and repeats the features of the psychical world, but from a new angle because there is the other (Green 2000b, 47).

Clinical material

One of D.W. Winnicott's (1999) formulations of gender is found in his discussion on the origins of creativity, where he suggests a paradox within the transit between femininity and masculinity, between the analyst and the analysand, and between aggression and frustration. Whereas Klein and Riviere highlight the inner world of anxiety, Winnicott's approach is through observing play as the potential space for symbolising the inner and external world (Abram 2008). He is famous for his critical quip, 'there is no such thing as the baby', a needed reminder to psychoanalysts that cultural life and the other create the capacity to be a baby whose right is to be as ruthless as it pleases. His idea of ruthlessness concerns the use of the object and this brings him to thoughts on aggression. Destruction, he believes, allows for creativity, provided that the other can stand the baby as a baby. Here is where the fact of dependency belongs to the other who can survive, without having to retaliate against the condition of being depended upon. In speaking about Winnicott's contribution to psychoanalysis, Pontalis observes that his notion of creativity 'is the condition for an exchange between inside and outside' (1981, 140).

Winnicott understands the problem of love, hate, and aggression through the uses rather than the ontology of the object. Object use presupposes the other and a shared environment. Because there is no environment without tension and frustration, the child's aggression is first and foremost a communication to the environment that must fail. Destruction must take place at two levels: the infant's omnipotence and the environment's omnipotence (Scarfone 2005). The paradox is that the environment must frustrate the child but not so much that the child loses hope in her or his own capacity to find and create the world that already exists. No aggression, Winnicott thought, was a sign of compliance, a giving up on the idea that playing with reality is an activity of the mind needed to release gender phantasy from the rigidity of the inner and outer world.

When reading Winnicott's paper on creativity, which contains quite a mad narrative of the inner world of gender, I found myself asking, what kind of man is Winnicott? And so I went to Joyce McDougall's lecture, 'Donald Winnicott the Man: Reflections and Recollections' (McDougall and Winnicott Clinic of Psychotherapy 2003). I suppose I was asking whether he, too, was a good enough mother. In a short vignette, McDougall asked Winnicott about his article called 'Hate in the Counter-transference'. There, Winnicott (1992) suggested why mother must hate the baby, or hates the fact that her omnipotence is of no use. McDougall (2003) wondered how he managed to support deeply disturbed patients that attacked his interpretations and refused to take anything he offered.

> Winnicott replied: 'We must admit that it is always fatiguing to be a bad breast.' He went on to explain that it was also very important that the bad breast analyst survived the attacks of the enraged infant within ... I sometimes wondered if perhaps he very much wished to be loved by his patients. (2003, 35)

It really is quite mad to understand that within the bad breast lives an enraged infant. And yet, the wish to be loved originates our capacity for both primal projections and our interest in self-understanding.

Winnicott's (1999) paper on the origin of creativity provides another sense of the difficulty of putting the question of gender to the analysand whose own questions are incredibility congealed. Indeed, he speaks of gender as hidden, as secret, and as repressed. And this leads Winnicott to write a very long sentence that indicates the slowness of psychoanalytic technique, followed by a short sentence on its limits:

> While it is the patient who is all the time teaching the analyst, the analyst should be able to know, theoretically, about the matters that concern the deepest or most central features of personality, else he may fail to recognize and meet new demands on his understanding and technique when at long last the patient is able to bring deeply buried matters into the content of the transference, thereby affording opportunity for mutative interpretation. The analyst, by interpreting, shows how much and how little of the patient's communication he is able to receive. (Winnicott 1999, 72)

Winnicott then describes his work with a married man of middle age who had had many experiences with therapy, including psychoanalysis, but was left with the feeling that something had been missed. In one session, Winnicott felt something new: the patient was speaking about his penis envy.

> I said to him: 'I am listening to a girl. I know perfectly well that you are a man but I am listening to a girl, and I am talking to a girl. I am telling this girl: "You are talking about penis envy."' (1999, 73)

Now Winnicott understood his interpretation as akin to playing with reality. His patient replied: 'If I were to tell someone about this girl I would be called mad' (1999, 73). But Winnicott went even further in this cross-identification when he then said to his patient: '"It is not that *you* told this to anyone; it is *I* who see the girl and hear a girl talking, when actually there is a man on my couch. The mad person is *myself*"' (1999, 74).

The interpretation introduces separateness: two people are in the same room but have different minds. It is at this point that the patient could then feel sane in a mad environment. This led to something deeper, for in the analytic work the patient felt (but without any proof) that his mother wished for a girl and could not see him as a boy. And in the strange logic of the unconscious, the man could not feel himself as a man. As for the cross-identification, Winnicott occupied the position of the patient's mother who was mad enough to see a girl when there was a boy. However, a few days later the patient fell ill and Winnicott began to think of what he called, for lack of a better term, 'the split off girl element in the male patient' (1999, 77).

The paper on creativity gets stranger. Winnicott brings to the clinical material a brief note on Shakespeare's *Hamlet* to illustrate gender dissociation. Even as he summarises the play, Winnicott cannot help giving Hamlet some stage directions, knowing full well that the character Hamlet would not be able to go to his own play. Hamlet's question – 'To be or not to be?' gives Winnicott a way to say something about the play and the disorder between 'being' and 'doing'. Even if Hamlet cannot decide whether he should or can exist, he is still only one person. Winnicott links 'being', or the capacity to know one's own existence, as a consequence of identification with the mother. 'Being', or what he calls the girl element, is the condition needed for the baby to enjoy fusing with the mother's femininity. It is the precondition for any self. While 'being' comes before 'doing', 'doing' allows for separation. Winnicott links the actions of 'doing' to the boy element, or the masculine position. Separation, Winnicott notes, also contains a deep-seated envy of femininity. This leads to a further astounding claim, because both doing and being contain elements of aggression, albeit of a different nature. 'It seems', writes Winnicott, 'that frustration belongs to satisfaction-seeking. To the experience of being belongs something else, not frustration, but maiming' (1999, 81). Frustration is an inevitable consequence of searching for satisfaction. Maiming is the reaching for existence that involves pushing against objects and therefore incurs both an emotional injury that provides one's place and the pleasure of feeling one's place. In Winnicott's view, the object survives this needed ruthlessness.

This formulation defied my expectation, which is to say, stereotypes that, however much I try to rid myself of them, seem to be reading me and so return as anxiety. I worried that Winnicott, or really, that I, might fall into a rhapsodic view of oceanic femininity, as a unifying force, while masculinity is relegated to discord. And if this is the separation, then only one element was aggressive, only one element valued. But it turns out that 'being' not only signifies being with someone – Winnicott's good enough mother – but someone who survives the baby's ruthless attempts at both unity and separation. These ruthless attempts to become a self are what Winnicott calls 'maiming'. Maiming comes before frustration, which sounds a different chord of aggression than the one played by Klein and Riviere. Maiming is now tied to creativity, to pressing on the world and not to hate, which, for Winnicott, comes much later and is rooted in frustration. The infant will create, from the world presented, what is already there. For the time being, the infant may act as if it can be the author of the world, but will soon come to be disillusioned by the mother's maiming, her being. Creating, finding, destroying, refinding belong to gender activity.

Winnicott's ideas about the poesis of gender bring a new understanding of the ripples of dependency, not only as an index of our profound helplessness, although we all begin there, but as a condition located on the borderline of being and doing, between the boy and girl element, and between the self and the other. He presents an emerging subject who finds and creates his or her being through maiming and doing, but without knowing it cannot be its own origin. Winnicott proposes this aggression, stemming from omnipotent thought, as gender's playground and mad scene. At first, the good enough mother provides the infant the conditions to discover, create, find, destroy, and so use what already exists. This permissiveness belongs to the mother's madness. To play with this reality, one must separate from reality. Such play involves a destruction of compliance, itself a reaction to cultural, social, and emotional impingement. The activity of this little destruction neither splits the self or the Other but rather is akin to what Winnicott names as 'maiming', a word we might use when conceptualising the transference field between the boy and girl element in any gender.

From Winnicott's clinical example comes the idea that splitting and the hostility toward male and female elements within any gender will agonise the subject's capacity for taking gender pleasure. He attributes these gendered elements as emerging from the human's constitutional bisexuality, and so gender becomes a commentary on the polymorphous nature of desire and object use, and then associated with something that is not gender at all, but still leans upon bodily activity, namely the capacity to be ruthless in playing with reality. I think Winnicott is suggesting that the afterlife of gender constantly constructs and deconstructs our own otherness that must include what is historical about the history of feeling the struggle to be a subject with other subjects. The paradox is that gender both registers the body as other and services the potential space with others. On this view, gender is always active and passive and signifies being and doing. Gender is found before it can be created. Yet the psychic cost of reducing gender to the encasements of biology, stereotype, or even knowledge is depression and rigidity, which translates into a defended organisation dedicated to hatred toward the self and the other, a wearing away in the faith that language can matter, and a giving up on the creative work of playing with reality. This is also the condition of war.

Lecture madness

In a lecture given to social workers, Winnicott offers a definition of illness: 'Let me use my friend the late John Rickman's definition: "Mental illness consists in not being able to find anyone who can stand you"' (1996a, 218). His definition may have resonance for everyday life, but it can also be used to return us to the problem of giving lectures on gender. If our lectures implicitly split off masculinity and femininity and only take one side of gender, it is as if we are telling the other side, 'no one can stand you'. We miss the opportunity to grapple with the relation of psychological significance to gender's sounding and instead demand compliance with external reality, another condition for war. If, in our lectures, we reduce gender to behaviour and social attributes, we lose contact with the emotional situation of gender's overabundance of meanings, conflicts, and disavowals. Lost as well is our capacity to link the war within to the contemporary wars in our own time.

Later in this lecture Winnicott relates madness to what is most ordinary about life, telling the social workers:

> Think of casework as providing a human basket. Clients put all their eggs into one basket which is you ... They take a risk, and first they must test you to see if you may be able to prove sensitive and reliable or whether you have it in you to repeat the traumatic experiences of their past. [Now, here is where the mad part comes.] In a sense you are a frying-pan, with the frying process played backwards, so that you really do unscramble the scrambled eggs. (1996a, 227)

It's quite something to move behind the scenes of the madness of lecturing on gender. We risk our own madness in doing so. My logic throughout this discussion began with rehearsing the worries that a lecture might depress the audience. A psychoanalytic approach, however, begins with objections to the emotional world and considers the transfer of the personal into the political as one of its inevitable consequences. There was also a last plea that in lecturing on gender we learn to unscramble eggs, an activity that cannot really be accomplished. Nor can we be frying pan playing backward, though we can try to imagine what comes before the scramble of gender. Here again is the gender madness and perhaps a new worry that a lecture drives the audience mad, playing, as it must, in areas of fusion, confusion, maiming, and separation. Still, if we can tolerate these mad parts and become curious toward their scrambled play, I believe we can learn a great deal and not only about the madness of lecturing on our life in topic of gender. We may learn to speak the strange grammar of gender's emotional logic, become curious with what love, hate, and aggression have to do with it, and perhaps play with this knowledge as ruthlessly as it is made. This would be the new madness: conceptualising gender as potential space. The large question is whether education, too, can tolerate this indirection and so serve as gender's playground.

Acknowledgements
An earlier version of this paper was originally given as an invited keynote to the Gender and Education Association's 7th International Conference in London, 25–27 March 2009.

Notes
1. André Green takes on the old word of 'madness' this way: 'Rather than characterize it as a disorder of reason, one should on the contrary stress the affective passionate element which modifies the subject's relation to reality, electing a part or whole object, becoming more or less exclusively attached to it, reorganizing his perception of the world around it, and giving it a unique or irreplaceable aura by which the ego is captivated and alienated' (1986, 223). Its model is ordered by love, and the use of the term 'madness' in my essay follows along Green's lines of research.
2. The psychoanalytic idea of aggression is drawn from the Freudian view of the life and death drives and the sadomasochistic element in psychical life. It can be thought of as an unconscious wish to destroy the object, although the unconscious logic behind this wish takes great force from any experience of frustration given the human's long maturation process, primal dependency, and radical need for care. Aggression, however, is a needed element for identification and creativity. For a discussion of aggression in cultural life, see Freud (2002).
3. While it is beyond the scope of this paper, Riviere (1991b) further develops the emotional force of splitting masculinity and femininity when she writes about femininity as in conflict with intellectual desire that tends to be considered a masculine possession and in phantasy, a diminishment of femininity. One outcome of this symbolic collapse, she argues, is an exaggerated femininity, or 'a mask of womanliness to avert anxiety and retribution feared from men' (1991b, 91).

References
Abram, Jan. 2008. Donald Woods Winnicott (1896–1971): A brief introduction. *International Journal of Psychoanalysis* 89: 1189–217.
Bion, Wilfred R. 1993. *Second thoughts.* London: Karnac Books.
Britzman, Deborah. 2003. *After-education: Anna Freud, Melanie Klein and psychoanalytic histories of learning.* Albany: State University of New York Press.
Britzman, Deborah. 2009. *The very thought of education: Psychoanalysis and the impossible professions.* Albany: State University of New York Press.
Butler, Judith. 1990. *Gender trouble: Feminism and the subversion of identity.* New York: Routledge.
Freud, Sigmund. 2002. *Civilization and its discontents (1929).* Trans. David McLintock. New York: Penguin Books.
Green, André. 1986. *On private madness.* Madison, CT: International University Press.
Green, André. 2000a. Experience and thinking in analytic practice. In *André Green at the Squiggle Foundation,* ed. Jan Abram, 1–15. London: Karnac Books.
Green, André. 2000b. On thirdness. In *André Green at the Squiggle Foundation,* ed. Jan Abram, 39–68. London: Karnac Books.
Klein, Melanie. 1937. Love, guilt, and reparation. In *Love, hate and reparation: Two lectures,* by Melanie Klein and Joan Riviere, 57–119. London: Hogarth Press.
Klein, Melanie. 1975. Early stages of the Oedipus conflict (1928). In *Love, guilt and reparation and other works, 1921–1945,* 186–98. London: Hogarth Press.
Klein, Melanie, and Joan Riviere. 1937. *Love, hate and reparation: Two lectures.* London: Hogarth Press.
McDougall, Joyce, and Winnicott Clinic of Psychotherapy. 2003. *Donald Winnicott the man: Reflections and recollections.* The Donald Winnicott Memorial Lecture, 2002, 17–37. London: Karnac Books.

Mitchell, Juliet. 1998. Introduction to Melanie Klein. In *Reading Melanie Klein*, ed. John Phillips and Lyndsey Stonebridge, 83–113. New York: Routledge.
Pitt, Alice J. 2003. *The play of the personal: Psychoanalytic narratives of feminist education.* New York: Peter Lang.
Pontalis, J.-B. 1981. The birth and recognition of the 'self'. In *Frontiers in psychoanalysis: Between the dream and psychic pain,* trans. Catherine Cullen and Philip Cullen, 126–47. New York: International Universities Press.
Rickman, John. 1937. Preface to *Love, hate and reparation: Two lectures*, by Melanie Klein and Joan Riviere, v–vi. London: Hogarth Press.
Riviere, Joan. 1937. Hate, greed, and aggression. In *Love, hate and reparation: Two lectures,* by Melanie Klein and Joan Riviere, 1–53. London: Hogarth Press.
Riviere, Joan. 1991a. The bereaved wife (1945). In *The inner world and Joan Riviere: Collected papers, 1920–1958,* ed. Athol Hughes, 214–26. London: Karnac Books.
Riviere, Joan. 1991b. Womanliness as masquerade (1929). In *The inner world and Joan Riviere: Collected papers, 1920–1958,* ed. Athol Hughes, 90–101. London: Karnac Books.
Rose, Jacqueline. 1993. *Why war? – Psychoanalysis, politics, and the return to Melanie Klein.* Oxford: Blackwell.
Scarfone, Dominique. 2005. Laplanche and Winnicott meet ... and survive. In *Sex and sexuality: Winnicottian perspectives,* ed. Lesley Caldwell, 33–54. London: Karnac.
Winnicott, D.W. 1992. Hate in the countertransference (1947). In *Through paediatrics to psycho-analysis: Collected papers,* 194–203. New York: Brunner/Mazel Publishers.
Winnicott, D.W. 1996a. Casework and mental illness (1963). In *The maturational processes and the facilitating environment: Studies in the theory of emotional development,* 217–29. Madison, CT: International Universities Press.
Winnicott, D.W. 1996b. A personal view of the Kleinian contribution (1962). In *The maturational processes and the facilitating environment: Studies in the theory of emotional development,* 171–8. Madison, CT: International Universities Press.
Winnicott, D.W. 1999. Creativity and its origins. In *Playing and reality,* 65–85. London: Routledge.

Intersectionality, Black British feminism and resistance in education: a roundtable discussion

Suki Ali, Heidi Mirza, Ann Phoenix and Jessica Ringrose (Chair)

> This roundtable discussion was the opening plenary panel of the 7th Gender and Education Association Conference, entitled 'Regulation and Resistance', held at the Institute of Education, London, 25–27 March 2009. The discussion centred on exploring the historical development and continuing relevance of intersectional and Black British feminist approaches for contemporary debates in gender and education.

Jessica Ringrose: OK, so the point of the panel today is to ask what is Black British feminism; and to think about the idea of intersectionality and of resistance *vis-à-vis* education. Kimberle Crenshaw, a Black feminist working in law in the US, coined the notion of intersectionality (Crenshaw 1989). She suggested, in 1989, the intersectional approach, 'aims to bring together the different aspects of an otherwise divided sensibility. And intersectional analysis argues that racial and sexual subordination mutually reinforcing'. Patricia Hill Collins, also a US Black feminist scholar describes intersectionality in a similar way, adding in more terms of reference, which I have found extremely useful in my own work. She says 'As a heuristic device ... [that] references the ability of social phenomena such as race, class, and gender to mutually construct one another. One can use the framework of intersectionality to think through social institutions, organizational structures, patterns of social interactions and other social practices on all levels of social organization' (Hill Collins 1998, 205).

Jessica Ringrose: Before I start the questions, I wanted to say something about the fact that I am a white woman chairing the panel. I benefit from my white racialisation and privilege, but its Black feminism that actually has allowed me to grapple with the intersectionalities of my own positionality. Black feminism is all about the politics of location, and enabling self-reflection on these issues. In planning the session we talked about the fact that actually having a white woman chair this session is working towards a politics of coalition, which we are going to be debating as we go on. But I think that maybe we tend to forget, particularly those of us sitting in the post-structural feminist camp, that it is actually Black feminist theory that is the *theoretical* anchor for a lot of these types of analyses. It insists on the politics of location, insists that we look at how race, class, and sexuality and gender work together, to constitute subjects. This cannot be add-on. It's got to be an integral part of our scholarship if we are going to have politically relevant scholarship and education.

Jessica Ringrose: The panellists' work has been guided by incredibly powerful questions, including: what are the experiences of success and failure for Black British girls and women in UK education? (Heidi) What are the psychic costs of racism and of sexualised racialisation for young people in UK schools today, and historically? (Ann) And what does it mean to be a girl in the context of UK schooling, for those constituted as mixed-raced feminine subjects? (Suki) They've all offered extremely powerful accounts of lived experiences through their empirical research. But there are some lingering questions about Black feminism: Can a feminism signified as Black be adequately inclusive? That's a provocative question. I am raising it purposefully to be provocative. Is its oppositional stance useful? Intersectionality, which is a guiding concept in some Black feminist work, has also been critiqued for producing models that are just multiplying oppressions or adding on oppressions to one another. Take the possibly problematic types of models where we have overly deterministic structural analysis of crossing roads, or very fixed subject positions that can't account for change. So then, what versions of intersectionality do we use?

Jessica Ringrose: The panel will also raise questions about resistance in education. What do we mean by resistance? Is it conscious, active? Is it a collective form of organised resistance? What about issues of internal psychic resistance in the face of our desires to change our own attachments, to injurious norms of racialisation and otherisation. What is also up for debate today is what forms of Black feminism will work for us in an increasingly 'post-feminist' popular cultural context; where gender and race politics play out in a lot of educational debates in ways that narrate girls as universally more successful than boys at school, and therefore in wider social spheres, or suggest that the real victims of post-industrial decline and economic crisis are white male working-class students and workers, for example. So in this supposedly post-class, post-race, post-gender, post-identity kind of world, what role is Black feminism playing? These issues are debated in a recent special issue of the journal *Race Ethnicity and Education*, entitled 'Black Feminism and Post Colonial Paradigms', which Heidi edited, and she narrates this really powerful story about inviting colleagues to contribute, and a young Black feminist colleague responded by saying – 'Thank you for organising this, I thought Black feminism was dead!' Suki responds in her article asking – what is the 'value added' for Black feminism in today's academy? What kind of course or theory is past its 'sell by' date?

Suki Ali: I would just like to clarify that I am not asking a question about value added because I am invested in that kind of managerial speak. I am rather thinking that that is the kind of marketisation model within which we work, and so I pose that question, actually, as a way of understanding one of the forms of regulation for Black feminism in the academy at the moment. And I suppose my responses were thinking about the ways in which Black feminism, as an umbrella term for our analyses, and how it might be important to think about where Black feminist theory is situated, where Black feminists, as embodied subjects, as teacher practitioners, are situated. And Black feminism as a kind of political project. And how the three aspects of what we might call, collectively, a form of Black feminism, are actually under different kinds of pressures and perhaps have different opportunities, actually, not starting on a completely negative note, opened up to them. So just to be clear that I am not invoking the value added as a useful way of thinking about these things. But it seems to me that, increasingly, the experience of trying to engage with Black feminism in the academy in different forms is one that's over-determined by the market model. And that has all sorts of implications for us as practitioners and teachers, for our students and for the work itself.

Heidi Mirza: It was very interesting to have this young woman say to me, you know I thought Black feminism was dead. And I suppose if you had asked me 10 years ago if I'd be sitting on a stage talking about Black feminism I would probably have said no. I remember about 10 years ago working at South Bank University, and the Vice Chancellor there said to me – Heidi, what are you doing these days? And I said, I'd just written a book on Black British feminism. He said – isn't it time that you grew up and got a proper career where you were taken seriously? And I suppose there has been this idea that looking at issues from a Black feminist perspective is somehow marginal … but the idea of a notion of Black that is homogenous is problematic. Black is a political space, because if you look at us on the stage we are from a range of different ethnic backgrounds, yet we self-identify with the notion of Black, is something that I've been told by my African American colleagues in the USA, that it's something quite specific to the UK, that we use a political umbrella of the space of blackness as something that we can identify with. And I think that's something that has come out of our post-colonial histories, and our post-colonial struggles here, in Britain, where we have been in so-called minorities, and hence our title. We might be global majority populations but we are actually seen as global minorities. And I think, you know, this debate about the term Black, who belongs and who doesn't, is a healthy one, if not sometimes a problematic one, and maybe we can discuss that a little bit here today, about that space, and the way that perhaps it's seen as falling away, or that it has fallen away to some extent, with the kind of neo-liberal discourses that we now engage in, which is more, much more, about our individual achievements and our individual strengths, and how we've overcome those things in our lives. And the increasing fragmentation and atomisation of our lives, as academics, and as, you know, students, and as employees. And religion has been ascendant as well, in a lot of our discourses about difference. And so the term Black, which is seen as an essentialised and problematic term has, to some extent, fallen away. And as well we've seen the ascendancy, as well, of terms like diversity, and it's, as Stuart Hall says, a highly problematic term, as it disavows racism. We talk about ethnicity and cultural difference, but we don't actually talk about race and racism quite in the same way. Although it is very much, as what's happened to Grace Livingstone,[1] still very much a part of our lives and the way that we are constructed. And the way that the nation state seeks to other those who are deemed as non-citizens, and non-humans if you don't have citizenship. So there is a way in which Black has now morphed, if you like, into a much more complex discussion of religion and identity and difference in a political and social arena. So I still want, however, to hold on to the notion of Black. And I know Jessica has voiced concerns about being a white woman on the stage, and I said to her – 'it's alright, you is Black!'. You know Ali G. Those of you who don't live in the UK, we have somebody called Ali G, who is white and Jewish, and plays a Black character. So my argument, really, is that we should still hold on to a political notion of Black. And I do worry that, as that young woman said, that it's something that is increasingly fading away.

Ann Phoenix: I am very interested in putting together a few of the comments that my colleagues have made just now. Because in trying to think about Black feminism and the way in which it's been influential and continues to be influential, for me the notion of intersectionality is absolutely key. And as Jessica said, when Kimberle Crenshaw coined the term in 1989 she was attempting to get at the ways in which nobody is ever located only in one category. We are all always multiply located, and the different categories to which we belong decentre each other, but always operate together, so that nobody is ever one gender position, one racialised position and so on. And it's not surprising that Kimberle Crenshaw is a Black US woman, working in law, who found that coining the term, to reflect on something that people were already thinking about, was important. Why I think those things go together, Black feminism and intersectionality, even before the term itself was coined, is because of the nature of experiences that people were having. So when Suki talks to us now about value added and although it's an economistic and neo-liberal term in many ways, if we go back to 1980, when I was a PhD student at Manchester and attempted to open a bank account, what happened to me was that the bank manager said that I had to show my passport. And I said – why? I've never shown a passport before to open a bank account, I am British, why should I? Who shows their passports? I was so angry I didn't stay there. I went to another bank, and they asked whether I was married. And I said I was, and they said I couldn't open it in the name of Phoenix but I had to open it in the name of my husband. And I was already in such a worn down state that I actually did. So for me that indicated one of the reasons why a Black feminist project was absolutely crucial, and why one had to think about racialisation and gender simultaneously, why they weren't separate.

Ann Phoenix: The example of Grace Livingstone, the other Black keynote being held at Heathrow and then sent back to the USA, shows that 20-odd years on, well almost 30 years, that we still need to think about the ways in which racialisation, nation, gender, all operate together to be regulatory, to actually discipline the embodied subjects that Suki talked about. So, for me, it's not possible to think about Black feminism without thinking about intersectionality. And it's also crucial to recognise that Black feminism, although it was often portrayed, certainly initially, as essentialist, exclusionary, many white feminists, white men, Black men, were very angry about the notion of Black feminism, but I think it never was exclusionary, it was an inclusionary project. It was quietly saying – look, we, in our multiplicities are here as well. But it was also saying this is a mode of thinking, this is a way of understanding the social world. And I think that that is really crucial. And to think about the specifically British context, I think that it's interesting that the organisation that was really key in the 1980s for Black feminists was the Organisation of Women of African and Asian Descent, initially, and then changed to the organisation of Women of African and Asian Descent, rather than something more narrow. So I would argue multiplicity has always been at the heart of, thinking of this particular politics of location.

Suki Ali: I would agree with that. And I would also agree that that is one of the narratives of feminism that's problematic, is the idea that our politics of identity is intrinsically about some form of essentialisation, rather than thinking about the politics part of what constitutes identity, and that also there's another tendency to sort of narrativise Black feminism as critique. And that, in itself, also collectivises and fixes the multiplicity of Black feminisms and takes a central, a kind of white feminism, white liberal feminism. There is a white western liberal feminism that dominates, and actually I think that does a disservice, in fact, to the multiple voices that we were constructing. OK? There's a centre, there are certain articulations of power and access to resources and positions within certain kinds of institutions, inevitably, but that the dialogue between feminisms was a crucial part, not a kind of failure, something to do with hostility, but an absolutely crucial part of the productive, creative, generative nature of multiple forms of serialisation, in much the way that you are saying. And we think about the, as you mentioned before, the Black collective and so on, and these are women of colour, queer women of colour, straight women, women talking about class, and this was really an important part of that work, so I mean I would certainly agree with that.

Heidi Mirza: I think that one of the interesting debates around intersectionality has been to what extent has it been a kind of limiting project as well. And limiting only in the terms that it is seen as, in a lot of the post-structural analysis, in terms of it being quite a structural, as opposed to post-structural model of how race, class and gender come together in women's lives. And I'll explain a bit what I mean by that. In Kimberle Crenshaw's model she uses the metaphor of avenues and traffic lights, and she talks about power, whether that's post-colonial power, gender power, race power, and disempowerment, running along particular avenues. If you can imagine huge roads meeting, and at the traffic lights, at the intersections you have traffic lights, so you can be going along a particular road, for example, gender, gender might be structuring your life, you might be in a relationship that's very limiting, you are not getting the employment opportunities because of your gender, you might be subject to domestic violence, you could be a trafficked woman that's been brought with little or no rights at all, from a southern country to a western country. You might have gender structuring your life, or you might have race structuring your life, because you could come, as I say, from a southern country, where there is poverty, and that has driven certain economic dynamic, which has resulted in why you were here in the UK. So you could have a situation where sexuality, gender, post-coloniality in that example as well, would all be elements that actually explain why that person is here and the kind of experiences that they are having, of oppression and disadvantage and marginality. And I particularly like that model and I think it's a strong model, because in the Black feminisms that I particularly find attractive, the economic and the structural inequalities women face somehow determines their experiences. So I do find that the explanation grounded in the kind of structural a useful concept for me to understand what's happening, particularly for young Black women in schools, systems of oppression, systems of disadvantage, roads or avenues of disadvantage, are quite important, I think, in explaining why we have persistent inequalities.

Jessica Ringrose: This leads us into the whole question of resistance. Because this whole debate is around whether a structuring and deterministic kind of model allow for fluidities, allow for change – allow for us to understand how social transformation's happening? And all of you have dealt really powerfully with questions of resistance in different ways. I mean, Heidi's work goes a long way in theorising Black women's struggles, and survival in higher education as a mode of resistance, rather than a mode of collusion into white dominant paradigms, for example. Ann's work has looked at processes of subjectivication and used psychosocial approaches, which have been so powerful for many of us. Suki, you know that I am fascinated by the way that you take up the visual to talk about both representation and the possibilities of re-signification.

Suki Ali: I want to go back to the idea of regulation first, and the ways in which different terms like intersectionality might be a more useful way of thinking about structural issues for something like diversity, I suppose. That's a common way of thinking about the diversity being, possibly even mix the blandness of the equal and equivalent forms of oppression. But I feel that intersectionality might be prey to that kind of critique as well, in fact, that these roads are just running along.

Ann Phoenix: I just think that that model has been one that has been much critiqued of the crossroads, and I think in mapping the margins in 1994, Crenshaw really fell prey to using that model. And many people don't theorise intersectionality like that, because A the roads are not fixed like that, and if you are going to theorise it like that you'd have to see them as dynamic as well as the traffic … I mean, it's just far too fixed and simplistic. And what is much more productive is the notion of mutual constitution. And that what you are calling the structural constituting itself as well as, you know, subjectivities and so on. So coming on to the multiple levels … there are lots and lots of people who wouldn't theorise intersectionality that way, and I don't think that would be productive. And, you know, for example, Baukje Prins in a 2006 article in a special issue of the *European Journal of Women's Studies*, on intersectionality talks about the division between what she calls systemic intersectionality, which she says is very much from the United States, where people are much more concerned with that sort of model of the structural; and the constructionist, which she sees as much more from the UK, which is much more likely to draw on post-structuralist type ideas.

Suki Ali: That's fine. In fact I would agree with you. I am sure we can have a disagreement as well, at some point, we are not going to agree about everything. The point I am making is there is a kind of way in which certain understanding of structural overpowering certain other forms of inequalities is problematic, and the idea that all structures impact equally, always, on individuals in the same way, is problematic, and a mutual constitution of certain kinds of inequalities is a more productive way of thinking about that. But whether we think of systems and subjectivities as separate in quite that way, is, of course, the bit that is problematic. And it is the articulation, as Stuart Hall might say when he engages with the idea of articulation of certain kinds of differences. And by that he means where they literally come together, but they might also be decoupled at certain points, for certain purposes, I think is quite important. And my kind of point then about resistance is … my sense of how we think about resisting then, whether we invoke terms like intersectionality or not, to me there is something really important about collectivisation and about dialogue. One of the things that Heidi talked about was the retention of a political notion of Black, a decoupling of blackness from a simple kind of ontology, or more yet a kind of practice, necessarily. If we think about Black feminism invoking a particular kind of political project that involves both practices and processes, then it becomes a sign under which we can collectively organise. I think this is a really key part of that core resistance. And Heidi talked about this in terms of individualisation, which I think is one of the major forces against this kind of connectivisation. So on the one hand, we are encouraged to be collaborative, in work and in higher education, and in other areas of education teamwork and collaboration is terribly important, but on the other hand, we are rewarded for increasingly individualated, increasingly individualised ways, on our performance. So for me this question of how we actually engage in collective practice and what collectivisation means and what collaboration means, is a theory that's kind of really pressing, and that the forms that takes might be different than they were 20 or 30 years ago. The kinds of dialogue that are being had are, necessarily, in some ways, different. But perhaps one of the things you touched on was the post-colonial perspective, about the ways in which it's important to think about history as of the present, the continuities and discontinuities, the points at which we recognise certain continued forms of inequality and regulation are transformed. Those are the things that I think are important. I'm not saying I've got an answer to that, necessarily.

Heidi Mirza: I want to go back to the point that you've made about intersectionality and the kind of structural model, because I think the importance, or for me, what really makes Black feminism something that works as an analysis and as a framework and as a theoretical paradigm, is the way in which agency and structure comes together. So on the one side, yes, we do have this model of the Kimberle Crenshaw intersectionality and avenues, which is quite clumsy and very difficult to actually operationalise, but on the other hand, the work that I've been doing, and I know both of you have, also, is looking at the embodied experience of people who are racialised, sexualised, classed, and age, disability, all those aspects shape their lives. So I think this idea of looking at intersectionality, bringing structure and agencies together, through an intersectional analysis that looks at embodied difference is really where, for me, Black feminism works.

Heidi Mirza: I can give you an example. I've been looking at the experiences of women in higher education, and particularly looking at the very early suffragette movement, and even those times in the turn of the century, there were Indian women suffragettes, something that's totally erased from history. And why they were important was they were the first women of colour to go to university in the UK from India. But although they were politically active, although they were pioneers, they have been erased from history, from our collective memory, from our understanding of the position of Black women in higher education. And as Spivak says, the experiences of these women, is as mute, visible, objects, so they would be quite visible, and in fact the Governor of India, when he saw them in the procession, the George V procession, where suffragettes were holding up banners, he talked about them as exotic creatures, you know, not as suffragettes, not as political and radical beings, but rather as people who had no agency, though they were expressing, indeed, tremendous agency. So I am really interested in looking at these hidden histories, which post-colonial feminists talk about as epistemic violence, this erasure, this non-existence of the other. And for me Black feminism gives me a framework to look at the agency of women, whether they are in school, whether they are in higher education, to draw on post-colonial historical contexts, so I can say listen, there is a past from which we can understand the present, and the way that racialised patterns and sexualised and gendered patterns reoccur, and sustain inequalities, for me that's why Black feminism is an important framework. So yes, I do agree that intersectionality can be top-heavy, but at the same time I think that we've transformed it with some of our theorising.

Ann Phoenix: I think the things that you've both said really chime with me. I particularly like the notion of thinking historically, and that's partly because I'm really, really keen on psychosocial analyses. So you talk about structure agency, which is a sociological version to some extent, but actually how important it is, always, to have the psychic and the social theorised together, never decontextualised, never apart. And when you say, Heidi, how things replay over time, I am very much struck by the Obama election, which has been talked about ad nausea. There is a really interesting piece by Kimberle Crenshaw and Eve Ensler, which is called 'Not in my Name', and what they are doing there, it seems to me, is intersectionality in the nicest possible way, and demonstrating why it's important, by pointing out that those white feminists who argued that, well, lots of people, that it's always the case that men, including Black men, get more privileges, earlier than women do, and therefore it was really important to elect Hilary Clinton rather than Barrack Obama, and it was reactionary and non-feminist to want to vote for Obama (Crenshaw and Ensler 2008). And what they are arguing is that, of course, that's overly simplistic, in so many ways. But there have been lots of pieces by surprising people sometimes, who tried to say that those who wanted Obama at the expense of Clinton were actually doing feminism a disservice, rather than recognising that there could be the first woman standing up against the first Black man standing, says a great deal about society in the first place, and that if you took an intersectional analysis it would not be so simplistic to say it's either his race or her gender being played off against one another in a simple way. So I think that that's really, really important, that we think about that, and think about it psychosocially.

Ann Phoenix: And to come on to something that you said, Suki, which is about seeing Black feminism as a sign. I really like that notion. And you've written about it as well, I like that notion that one thinks about Black feminism as signifying all sorts of progressive politics, and I think that that's important. And hence it makes it possible for Black feminism to have been something that inspired you, Jessica, for example, into thinking about intersectionality, and the way in which you wanted to do politics, and do research and so on, rather than seeing Black feminism as something exclusionary, that's something to do with chromatism. And resistance, to come back to your question, after a long way around, is seen in the way in which we theorise in an inclusionary manner. And I think that there's a real tension between different sorts of resistances that might be seen as, on the one hand, the post-race position which has gained fancy at the moment, which is saying, well, you know, forget blackness, forget race, it shouldn't matter, and indeed we know that it's the most trivial possible. And people are saying, well, we want to resist through recognising that racism still matters. And these two positions, it seems to me, have to be treated not as opposites, even though they seem completely opposed. And so it comes back to something that Heidi was saying about the importance of maintaining an interest in structure, while at the same time thinking about agency. And one of the things I write about, in the special issue, are Caribbean women who were serial migrants, they were left in the Caribbean when their parents came to Britain and then they joined them later, and I'm asking them to reflect backwards on that experience, and in fact what I write about in that piece about their school experience. One reason I think that that's a supreme example of psychosocial resistance is it demonstrates the ways in which memory is both a recuperation and dealing with the past, which is for the individual, but also social resistance, by saying that what happened was problematic. We are resisting that, and we want that story told in order that people can see that our story was valid, and what was done to a generation of African Caribbean children in British schools. So I think that it makes for muilti-level resistance. Angela Davies has argued a great deal that we need to think about multiple levels of analyses when we are thinking, for example, about intersectionality, and I would argue that we also need to do that about resistance.

Suki Ali: I want to touch on something else that's lurking around here about, sort of, you know, the difficulty of, Jessica raises, about essentialising ... And we talked about chromotism, and the difficulty of talking simply about chromotism. But my kind of Obama moment was when I saw an African American family walk out on to that dais.

It was a really profound moment for me, when that actually happened. Or the Slumdog Millionaire moment, which was painful in many ways, but when the Oscar's stage was filled with people from the South Asian sub-continent. These kind of moments, really, for me, we've talked about that relationship in relation to embodied difference, and being careful about talking about that embodied difference as race, as racialisation, as chromotism, are quite tricky. Because I think that if we think about Black feminism as being founded on discussions around experience, experience as constituted of subjects, rather than subjects having experiences, to borrow from James Gott, then these kind of paradoxes around visibility, hyper-visibility, and invisibility, and how they do relate to certain kinds of bodies, as Nirwal Puwar talked about 'space invaders' invading certain kinds of white space, these are the things that start to become quite difficult. That what you are pointing to, I think, is that an intersectional analysis has to be able to incorporate both of those. So it's not about a kind of re-ontologisation, or a kind of essentialisation of that Black experience, but a recognition that to be a Black feminist in the academy, to be embodied as such, to be visible as such, is something that impacts on one's experience, that constitutes oneself, through these, that is a form of subjectivisation, it's often a form of regulation, actually, and also must be a site of resistance. How we actually deal with those complexities, I think, is another matter. But what we are saying is that there are sort of multiple ways of thinking about these issues. For most of us they are post-structural in the sense that structure still matters. One is not abandoning a structural analysis and the sense that material conditions matter to those debates, at the same time is looking to deconstruct how those operate, and to look at the performative and discursive aspects of those encounters, which are really important.

Heidi Mirza: I think that the early work of Amina Mama in *Feminist Review* in the early 1980s, when she talks about migrant women in the health service, in catering, in locating particular places in the economy. And if you are talking about higher education, and we are talking about the numbers, and the visibility, and the hyper-visibility, of Black and minority ethnic people in higher education, they are in catering, they are the cleaners. They are not the lecturers, and they are some of the students, but mostly overseas students. So I go back again to the way that we would have experiences as, Ann and I, two of the few Black professors in the UK, I think at the last count there were 15 Black women professors. So, you know, there is a sense in which we are still talking about visibility and embodiment, and the subjective experiences that we have, as a consequence, is largely shaped by people's broader, normal, expectations of where you should inhabit, and places that you should be. What is right and proper?

Heidi Mirza: I remember when I was first promoted to a senior lecturer, and I had a position on the research committee, again going back to my time at South Bank, and again, my favourite Vice Chancellor, as I walked into the room, he thought I was the coffee lady, and when I didn't serve the coffee and he realised I was sitting down, like everyone else, he then asked me what my husband did, going back to points about husbands determining your social location. So there gender, and race, as we have been talking, with the banks, do structure your experience, and you live an embodied experience as a consequence, so expectations that people have of us are always things that we have to overcome in our positions of relative power in the academy. So I do think that looking at resistance in terms of the scope that we have to resist always is contained, again, within these inequalities that are very apparent and very tangible about what is permissible and where you can go and what you can do.

Heidi Mirza: I am thinking about the resistance of the young African Caribbean girls in my early study of girls in schools in London, they resisted through a number of techniques that were quite inventive and imaginative. You know, at that time the most dominant social theory about resistance in schools was Paul Willis's book *Learning to Labour*, which was about working-class boys, and my book *Young Female and Black* was about Black working-class girls, and the paradigm that Paul Willis, the sort of theoretical framework was that the boys sort of resisted through rituals ... But what I found with my girls was that they weren't resisting as a political act, but they chose strategies about things that they knew. So, for example, they knew that certain opportunities weren't going to be open to them. They couldn't become a banker or a lawyer, because they knew that in their post-colonial history they knew that their parents weren't that, they didn't have those opportunities, and therefore they chose to resist quite quietly and subversively by ... maybe not ... listening to the teacher, staying at the back of the classroom, but they got on with work, because they also knew that doing well at school would give them certain opportunities. So there was a whole sense in which they had multiple layers of resistance where they weren't just simply, you know, storming out, joining a gang, and all of that, but were quiet and subversive. And another sort of dominant theory at the time was that girls did better than boys, Black girls did better than Black boys, and boys in general, because they were following the strong role models of their mother. Which was another problematic theory about resistance ... and again we have role models as a very prominent government policy at the moment for young Black boys, in order for them to become mentored and follow strong Black male role models in order to overcome a lot of the problems. But what I found was although girls talked about their mothers in very glowing terms, they weren't following in the paths of their mothers necessarily, but the experiences of their mothers were the only thing that they had to go on, because they didn't have the wider horizons, they were contained within class and schooling contexts where certain opportunities weren't open to them. So they would choose things like, yes, to be a nurse, but they would say over and over again – I don't want to be a nurse because I want to be like my mother, but I know I can get to college, that's why I am choosing that career. So there was a whole way in which they were resisting at multiple levels, beyond a lot of our theorisation.

Jessica Ringrose: In Suki's conclusions from the special issue she says 'I am convinced that there is a need for Black feminists to form alliances for and among themselves, as well as others. I do not know who might wish to include or exclude themselves from that term, but we should continue to use debate and dialogue to explore this. If we see Black feminism as a process that is formed through relationships and ideas, rather than as a fixed or stable sign or entity to return to the thing that we've been discussing, it allows us to continue to use the term, it's relevance to contemporary work is continually being renegotiated'. I think this statement is quite powerful, and I would like to turn it over now over to the audience to continue questions for the panellists about Black British feminism.

Question 1 (audience member): I wanted to ask a question about some of the unexpected turns or ways in which intersectionality has been used to talk about the marginalisation and or disadvantage of certain groups of men ... So an example would be that some Black men in the United States have used an intersectional analysis to claim the sort of marginalisation of working-class Black males, either in the academy or used intersectional analysis to claim that Black women are actually more advantaged over

Black men in the academy. Or even the way, sometimes even some of my colleagues try to talk about the invisibility of certain groups, working-class white students and kind of, again, using that as an intersectional analysis, or even at this conference the way intersectionality is invoked not necessarily to include race, class and gender, but sometimes to look at disability and class, or gender and nationality. So I'm wondering what, you know, should, in the name of Black feminism is there an intervention to be made? And or is that just one of the kind of unexpected turns that theory takes? Should there be, kind of, a response to that? It's something that concerns me because I think that there may need to be a response when intersectionality is used to further certain forms of oppression, rather than anti-oppressive practice and/or analysis.

Ann Phoenix: I think it's a great comment and question. I really like it, and it plays into various things that have been debated about intersectionality. One, for example, is Judith Butler talks about the over-signification that's, you know, and the sign of tiredness that's illustrated by the use of the word etc., Black working-class woman, you know, you can imagine, able bodied, the etc., she says, suggests a sign of sort of exhaustion, and it's inimitable signification. So when do you stop? How many categories would be enough? What are the intersections that one is looking at? And I think that intersectionality does call for looking at a whole range of different intersections, because people are multiply positioned in relation to all those things that you are talking about, sexuality, embodiedness, all those things as well as gender, race and class and so on. So that although, when it was first used Crenshaw saying – I want to name it in order to be able to look at gender and race together, it is open to being used in a number of different ways; we have to think about for what purpose are we doing particular analyses? And therefore do analyses around those things that matter, the things that are making a difference for whatever it is we are looking at. Actually recognising that by focusing on particular things we are excluding others, and that that can't be helped. So I think that that's important. She, herself, talks about in her work there are 14 things that she counts up, 14 categories that she looks at, and of course that doesn't exhaust the possibilities. Now, I don't think that one needs to say – I am looking at this, this, this and this. Nor do I think the etc. is actually a sign of exhaustion. I think it is a sign of recognition, which is something that Judith Butler would like very much, and that's OK, to be specific, to be situated in what one does.

Ann Phoenix: Now, then, in terms of using intersectionality in unexpected ways that you see as not progressive, you didn't use that term, but one might say, I think any language that is produced to deal with, whether Heidi calls it oppression, or to deal with differential positioning, to do with power relations, always gets used by those who see their power as being sort of usurped by people making a claim to the sort of power relations that put them in a more powerful, or slightly more powerful, position than they were in before. So I think that that's not unusual, that it would be used that way. And one of the things that I want to say quite strongly is that intersectional analysis is not about a hierarchy of oppression. So one of the things that you are talking about that people do in order to usurp claims to power is to say well actually, when you look at it we are more oppressed than they are. And I think that that's one of the things that intersectional analyses were designed to disrupt, to say that there's a, you know, an oppression Olympics, or a hierarchy of oppressions and so on, and that we really have to hold that line. Having said that, of course, I think that there are many ways in which Black working-class men in the United States and elsewhere are being subject to discriminations of all sorts, they really do need attention. Similarly, I would say the same goes for white working-class boys here sometimes, but that doesn't take away or devalue the importance of addressing racisms, for example, in all of their pluralities, and it doesn't mean, therefore that, as some people wanted to do, that one says that actually we've got it all wrong, what we should be doing is focusing all our educational attention on white working-class boys, because we now know that they are the ones who really need help, and no-one else. Because that is absolutely not in the script of intersectionality!

Heidi Mirza: Could I come back on the question as well? Again, I really think it was a good question, and I think it raises for me what we've talked about, which is that there are different ways in which different intersections or different aspects or isms happen at different historical times, and that some isms are more important to a particular group at a particular historical time than another, so for example we have a whole upheaval at the moment about the signification of race and masculinity embodied in Obama. So we have a sense in which there is this notion that we are now post-race and, you know, Black men are no longer in prisons, but of course they are in prisons, of course they are not getting the opportunities. Racism still exists. Yet, you know, in different historical times the manifestation of how we talk about race and masculinity will shift, so we are seeing, we are living through, quite an enormous shift at the moment, in the same way as we are living through an enormous shift about what is citizenship, as we can see with Grace Livingstone, about who matters and who doesn't matter. So I do like analysis, which talks about intersectionality as very fluid, and historically specific, and interpretative.

Suki Ali: You've asked a very important question, which is what happens to certain terms and theoretical constructs as they are taken up and mainstreamed. I guess this kind of comes back to my earlier question about what gets taught where, what gets used where, what gets valued as a useful approach? That there is nothing ever really inevitably liberating or anti-oppressive about anything that we do, in a way, or any kind of theoretical framework. And we need to invest these with a kind of politics, you know, whichever our politics is, let's say. I think one of the things we haven't talked about is the kind of shared politic projects, what our shared political projects are. That is a crucial issue, so that we might invoke intersectionality in ways that some consider to be problematic, because there's nothing intrinsically liberating about using that term or, 'diversity' or any of these other kind of buzz words. And watching where certain terms get taken over, where they get built up, where they shift from one terrain to another, I think, is a really important task for us.

Question 2 (audience member): As a paradigm we should remember that you need to search for data to support your paradigm. And we want to champion the paradigm, and I would say even the origin of intersectionality resulted from the fact that there was data out there that could not be identified by anything that existed at that time. So let's not get carried away, and forget that men may feel that they are not part of that paradigm, and I don't particularly think that white feminism is also, you know, it's kind of taking a secondary position, but the data may not, in particular instances, not always include Black feminism. So it has to fit, there has to be a fit, it has to be reasonable. It can't just be all things fit in one. We have to be social scientists and evaluate in a logical, reasonable, way.

Ann Phoenix: I think that's right, of course, but of course there's all sorts of data that demonstrates, you know, particular things at particular times, that different groups are disadvantaged.

Audience member: Oh, I am not saying that is not true, but which groups and which places? Are we going to have a complex causal analysis or pick something that you want to champion, as opposed to having it so complex, and it all has to be about intersectionality?

Heidi Mirza: Could I just say that also the groups though that we might collect data on change. So, for example, I am interested in the mixed-race group in the UK, for example, this is a group that has just recently been constituted in policy, and has become an object of study, and a site for pathologisation, intervention, at risk in many, many ways. So it requires us to think, as you say, to think carefully about the types of tools you want to bring to that, and the kinds of theory that we need to use, because this group simply did not exist before the census created, as it were, produced a particular group.

Audience member: But are Pacific Rim, Asian, other groups, are they going to identify with this paradigm?

Ann Phoenix: Well you talk about 'the paradigm'. It is a theoretical term that is meant to be able to illuminate, as all theoretical terms are, social conditions and circumstances. And I think one of the things that's useful about what you just said is to think, are we going to think complexly, or are we going to choose what we are going to campaign on and campaign on, and I think that brings us back to what Suki said, just towards the end, that we haven't talked about really, and we haven't talked about politics and the things we want to campaign about, and I think that we have to do both, we have to have a politics. And that's one of the things about feminism, that we all take for granted, sitting here, that it's also a politics of course, or several politics maybe, but certainly political.

Audience member: Yeah, but people are picking their politics.

Ann Phoenix: But we have to think complexly, theoretically, we really do! Because something that Wendy Holloway wrote once, that really strikes me, is that quite often our social science is much more simplistic than the lived, everyday practices and processes. So I think that we have to, actually, think complexly. But we also have to have strategic alliances, coalitions, that at times allow us to focus on particular politics that are feminist, that are racialised, and both at once, and that allow us to get social change. And I think that that's really important. That's an important clarion call, and we haven't said enough about that here.

Question 3 (audience member): The title that you've given is Black British feminism, and listening to you what I've heard is talk about something much more global. So I wonder if you could speak to the specificities of the Britishness of the Black feminism in the title, and how far we can go with that?

Heidi Mirza: Well, I think it returns to the point that we were just making about coalition and the way in which there's been, what I was saying, quite a unique history. I think I did this at the very beginning, there is quite a unique history in Britain, because of this way in which coalitions formed around being othered. The other day, I was re-reading Audrey Lord, *Sister Outsider*, and one of the things that really struck me is, and there was an analysis by Gail Lewis, and she was saying that the thing about the Black British couplet, is that the Black is the outsider, but the British is an insider position. So it is about the nation's state and actually belonging or the struggle to belong, and the struggle of what constitutes Britishness, which is an ongoing situation, but at the same time being Black, actually, is a statement about standing outside of that, and has allowed us to have very fruitful, contested, difficult, coalition politics. But I think, as my colleague over there has said, what has come out of it is again a contested notion of Black feminist theory, which, you know, is a feminisms in the plural, because there are many different views and aspects to that. There are post-colonial feminisms. I take a more structural materialistic, others take a more structuralist, so there are ways in which Black feminisms, and Black British feminisms, have evolved in a unique historical context.

Ann Phoenix: Well, yes, I would agree with that. I think that you raised an important question about the concerns around global and transnational thinking, about how they actually play out in practise, which echoes, I think, the previous questions. And actually it's really hard to speak to the terms in any meaningful way, on one level, when we are constantly struggling with that kind of transnational. But I think the Black and the British, as you rightly point out, inevitably are transnational and post-colonial, and therefore have a certain global reach to them in their very kind of historical constitution.

Heidi Mirza: It's disruptive as well. I know that Patricia Hill Collins came 10 years ago, when we published *Black British Feminism*, and it was quite unsettling that we had a notion of British that included Asian, South East Asian, a whole range of complex, mixed race, complex identities, because the collection of *Black British Feminism* included all these multiple positionings, and she wrote to me and she said – I've had to go away and think about what African American feminism means, in the context of what you are calling Black. So it was disruptive, it opened dialogue and debate, and some people do not want the term 'Black', we have ideas about Asian feminists, we have a sort of fragmentation going on, so we have 'Asian feminists', 'feminists of colour' is another term that's used, 'post-colonial feminists'. It's all fluid and moving, even as we speak.

Suki Ali: But I think it's important about how the kind of national context structures that. I think that's the point. So African American feminist approach for intersectionality, obviously evolves from a history of very structural forms of racist law making and policy and so on and so forth, and it's slightly different form to the British.

Ann Phoenix: I would just echo what Heidi and Suki said, and just add to it that that contestation around blackness, which has been so particular to the British context is what makes it Black British feminism actually. So that in the 1980s when we were fighting over who was Black, and who could be included in, and OWAD changed its name from Organisation of Women of Africa and African Descent to African and Asian descent, it was a big step. And then there were debates about, in fact, whether the Irish were Black in the British context, because for exactly the reasons that Asians were also Black, around racisms and it's plurality and their plurality and so on. Then that contestation that meant that many people stopped including Asians as Black again, in the British context ... So all that, I think, is peculiarly British and has led to particular British campaigns around Black British feminism. But I think also, as Heidi and Suki have both said, transnationalism is key, because of the, if you like, the closeness of Empire in history. So that when Paul Gilroy talks about post-colonial melancholia being written on the national psyche I think that that's important, also, to bear in mind, and it's particular again from what is the case, for example, in France, or the United States and so on. So there are all sorts of particularities that have led to particular coalitions here that make them Black, British, and Feminist.

Note

1. As described in the introduction to this special issue, Grace Livingstone, a Jamaican national who travels with a US Green Card, was another plenary panellist, scheduled to present at the GEA 2009 Conference. On the Saturday prior to the conference Grace was detained at Heathrow. Held for 11 hours, she was eventually refused entry and sent back to the USA. According to Grace, passport control refused to accept she was a keynote speaker at a UK university event.

References

Collins, Patricia Hill. 1998. *Fighting words: Black women and the search for justice*. Minneapolis: University of Minnesota Press.

Crenshaw, K. 1989. Demarginalizing the intersection of race and sex: A black feminist critique of antidiscrimination doctrine, feminist theory and antiracist politics. *University of Chicago Legal Forum* 139–167.

Crenshaw, K. and E. Ensler. 2008. http://www.huffingtonpost.com/...crenshaw...ensler/feminist-ultimatums-not-ib85165.html

Mirza, H. S. and C. Joseph (eds). 2009. Black feminisms and postcolonial paradigms: researching educational inequalities. *Race Ethnicity and Education* (special issue) 12, no. 1.

Prins, Baukje. 2006. Narrative accounts of origins: A blind spot in the intersectional approach? *European Journal of Women's Studies* 13, no. 3: 277–290.

Everyday banality in a documentary by teenage women: between the trivial and the extreme. Schooling and desiring in contexts of extreme urban poverty

Silvia Grinberg

Escuela de Humanidades, Universidad Nacional de San Martin, Conicet, Buenos Aires, Argentina

In this article, I offer some reflections on a video documentary workshop for students in the first year of middle school. The workshop, which was held in 2008, took place in a school in an area of extreme urban poverty in the metropolitan area of Buenos Aires, Argentina, specifically in one of the more and more common spaces usually called shantytowns. The students were asked to conceive of, produce and film a documentary video. The only restriction was that the project be about their daily life and not be fictional, because the project was constructed as an opportunity to create, in the context of the school, spaces for thinking about and problematising the world. The workshop itself and its product – a documentary about trash and waste in the neighbourhood – confront us with the fact that the material conditions of existence can never be isolated from desire and the will to live. Doing is always constituted in certain conditions of existence and, returning to Deleuze and Guattari, desire is always close to those conditions. This experience of doing entails the life of subjects, the dynamics of school life but also – and here I am going to speak of what these young women made, in which they express their interests, concerns, desires and aspirations – political statements insofar as an affirmation of life and the flows of desire.

Introduction

> Everyone thinks that Cárcova is a polluting place where strange people live, people who are strange because they are from there. But that's not true. I'm from there and I'm not strange. I'm way cool. (Nair, 13 years old)

As Britzman states in relation to the potential contribution of feminist pedagogy to pedagogy in general, there is something 'fundamentally scary about pedagogy because it references the unknown ... more often than not, things do not go according to plan' (1992, 151). She goes on, 'we can conclude that pedagogy ushers in an intangibility that we can identify as the "uncanny"' (1992, 151). Hence, Britzman points out that critical and feminist pedagogies, 'can help us return to these tangles in ways that move beyond the impulse to manage techniques, discipline bodies, and control outcomes' (1992, 151). This perspective opposes pedagogy to the institutional and the status quo. It also allows us to wonder about possibilities for resistance, power boundaries, as well as the voices and contradictions that can arise in schools and their relations. It is from this perspective that I will present the results of the research that I have been doing since 2004 in schools in contexts of extreme urban poverty in Greater Buenos Aires, Argentina. In keeping with Britzman's formulation, in this article I will try to evidence a sort of resistance to the authorisation of official meanings that circulate in the feminist classroom.

Some brief comments about the project that this article discusses. Initially, my work centred on the first years of schooling but, since 2007, I have been focused on middle school education. This is not a chance shift, and it has allowed me to observe and explore some of the dynamics of school life, dynamics that begin in elementary school and that, by middle school, have often led to violent explosions,[1] tremendous apathy, and everything in between. I believe that highly conflictive behaviour at the middle school level that is often considered part and parcel of a certain age is, in fact, an outbreak of dynamics that are established in the first years of elementary school. In this paper, though, rather than analyse the result of my research, I am concerned with discussing the experience of a documentary video workshop, held over the course of 2008, with teenagers in the first year of a middle school located near a shantytown. Although there is most certainly a continuum between my research and the workshop, here the focus is the documentary that these young women made. Similarly, though the images contained in the documentary are relevant to audiovisual ethnography (Araya Gomez 2003; Ardévol 1998; Pink 2008), that is not the approach I take here. The images, dialogues and opinions dealt with come from the documentary that these young students designed and filmed, and this analysis is guided by their voices, desires and perceptions.

First, I will offer a brief description of the workshop and the neighbourhood in which the school is located, followed by an in-depth discussion of the theoretical basis for the project, and finally some words on the video produced by these young women.

About the workshop, the video, the neighbourhood…

In brief, a shantytown is the territorial expression of the increase in marginality and extreme urban poverty in Latin America, particularly in Argentina. The occupation of the lands is individual: each family or individual arrives to the land on its own and builds its house as best it can; there is no urban organisation; there are no streets, just passageways. The lands are occupied illegally. The emergence of the shantytown can be traced back to the early twentieth century. The growth of this sort of space, which has been constant since the 1970s, has accelerated considerably, however, since the 1990s. In this context, the possibility of uprisings is always present; hence, social policy, through clientelism in the distribution of welfare plans, anticipates these upheavals, reducing the margins of discontent and, thus, the risk of social unrest. The shantytowns are areas full of people without legal documentation who arrive silently; as long as they do not cross the boundary and unsettle the outside world, they can wander the alleyways of the shantytown unbothered.

The workshop took place in a middle school located in one of the many areas of the Buenos Aires metropolitan areas that exemplifies the dramatic growth in shantytowns. Significantly, this workshop, which was planned jointly with the school principal, entailed weekly two-hour sessions during school hours. To varying degrees, Spanish language, history and science teachers also participated in it.

Although this project was initially proposed to the whole group of students, the women in the group were the ones who participated in the production (that is, the design and filming). As will be discussed in these pages, these young women were able to narrate their lives, concerns and desires in this video. Hence, this paper deals with the experience of teenage women in one of the largest shantytowns in the Buenos Aires metropolitan area. It discusses how within the school space they pick up and appropriate the camera to narrate their lives.

During the first months, the students worked on the selection of the topic and the script, and received basic training in camerawork, etc. During the second part of the school year, the young women went out to film. Both the material filmed and the planning of the video were the product of their decisions.[2] As a result, the crux of the project is the vision and words of these young women: what they showed and how they showed it, where they put the camera lens, what they decide to narrate in the video, etc.

The video, then, reflects these young women's daily life, their perspectives, thoughts, desires and perceptions. In this, the workshop, like the research, makes uses of de Certeau's (2007) approach to ways of operating that occur, take shape and are produced in the everyday life of territories, that is, the everyday life of subjects, neighbourhoods and institutions. At the level of school life, our interest lies in pedagogical devices and their forms; authorised modes of doing and saying (Britzman 1992), as well as teachers and students' improvised ways of doing and saying in non-official spaces that, through the workshop and the camera, we enabled. The daily contact with teachers and students that this work implied allowed us to approach both ways of exercising power and ways of contesting and resisting it, whether in the neighbourhood or in the school.

In a number of manners, those ways of operating express, assemble and articulate the changes that took place in the last decades of the twentieth century. I believe that these changes entail a tangle of issues that arise out of the virulence of the social, political, economic and, of course, educational transformations that took place in those years. Judging from their effects, the 1990s were quite clearly years of neo-liberalism; Latin America in general and Argentina in particular were by no means exempt from neo-liberal processes; indeed, they were factories, so to speak, of privatisation and of laws that, among other things, removed measures to protect employment, health care and education. I want to emphasise the notions of factory and of virulence because I believe that they map out the territory we are dealing with, the territory shown in this video by these young women. In one decade, the population of shantytowns grew exponentially and, hence, traumatically. Indeed, in countries like Argentina that, over the course of the twentieth century, had established very local versions of the welfare state in terms of the workings and development of the economy and of the educational system, the ways that subjects lived changed dramatically in a very few years. This is particularly true in the case of the educational system, to which the State had been crucial since the beginning. The Argentine educational system, and I mean each and every one of its schools, was created, economically supported (from teachers' salaries to chalk and paper), supervised and so forth by the federal government. This state of affairs was, once again, virulently modified by two laws:[3] one passed in the 1970s, in the midst of the military dictatorship, and another in the early 1990s. These laws automatically transferred responsibility for schools from the federal government to the provinces. This transferal occurred without also allocating to the provinces the financial resources that would enable them to handle the task. Indeed, the markings and effects of that process are still felt, observed and produced in the life of subjects and, of course, of institutions. Although the focus of this paper is not those processes,

I believe it is important to bear them in mind since they are key to what I am discussing here. I understand that it is possible to study these processes from a number of different perspectives: on the basis of governmental documents, of the specialised literature produced at a certain time and of the processes that take place in the territories themselves. In referring to processes and transformations in subjects' ways of operating (de Certeau 2007), I would like to clarify that I understand that, like a palimpsest with traces of memories of a wide range of types of life for both people and institutions, *doing* entails layers that come together to form a reality. Hence, ways of operating are constituted, created and produced in certain historical conditions; further, they can only be understood as the productions effected by subjects in a setting.[4] The video that I am analysing here was produced in the framework of a middle school and a territory that, in many ways, is the result of these policies. What these young women say and show in relation to their neighbourhood must be understood, I believe, as the effects of neo-liberalism in Latin America on the daily life of subjects.

Young people and desiring production

The workshop took place in the context of a research project framed by what could be called governmentality studies (Foucault 2006, 2007; Grinberg 2008; O'Malley 2007; Rose 1999; Rose, O'Malley, and Valverde 2006). The research deals with the processes of subjectivation as well as the production of identities in school space, heeding the ways that inequality is produced and reproduced. These concerns are evident, on the one hand, in studies into the process of formulation and implementation of neo-liberal educational reform in the late twentieth century and, on the other – and this is what I want to focus on here – on the processes and dynamics of everyday life in the neighbourhood and in the school.

As stated above, through governmentality studies, it is possible to approach both the dynamics by which power is exercised and processes of resistance and struggle in daily life. This, to return to O'Malley (2007), entails thinking about the multiple ways of doing effected by subjects and institutions. And that is a premise in the development of this workshop: working with students such that their word – that is, what concerns and interests them – is pivotal.

I suggest that school life in contexts of extreme urban poverty has come to take place between, on the one hand – and returning to Deleuze and Guattari (1995) – the abject fear produced by such poverty and its attendant negation and exclusion and, on the other, the young people who, having been born in these contexts, forge an image of affirmation and production that, for those who, first and foremost, want to stay out of such contexts, is hard to process.

Thus, as McNay points out (1992) in discussing the agency of women, we believe that this video expresses both the devices of power – the crystallisation on the ground of certain social configurations – and the creative potential of these young women that is able to non-schematically express situations of oppression as well as ways of subverting them.

It is important to discuss here the ways, procedures and mechanisms by which certain local and regional, as well as global, dynamics take shape in the life of people; that is, the way they produce subjectivity. Ways of operating that articulate the social transformations that have taken place in recent decades. I believe that that set of changes constitutes something more than just another variable to be analysed. Thus, speaking of processes of subjectivation means understanding that 'the subject is produced by historically varying conditions that are sustained by their produced elements' (Bell 2007, 11). As Deleuze and Guattari (2000) describe, the difference does not lie between the social and the individual: on the molecular level of desires and beliefs, that distinction, as they point out, makes no sense.

Here, through the voices of these teenage women we were able to evidence processes of subjectivation as well as the socio-historical conditions in which these young women were born and grew up. To return to Butler (2002), this entails the abject both in terms of the territory and those who live there; in this case, teenage women who live in the most neglected, denied and threatened spaces; the abject of the city.

The workshop itself as well as its product – a documentary video that the students made about trash and waste in the neighbourhood – confronts us with something that we all know but that is difficult to see and conceive: none of the material conditions of existence can be isolated from ways of operating or, significantly, from desire and the will to live. Doing is always constituted in certain conditions of life. To quote Deleuze and Guattari, 'Desire always remains in close touch with the conditions of objective existence; it embraces them and follows them, it shifts when they shift and does not outlive them' (1995, 34). This is the framework in which these theorists discuss the distinction between the social production of reality and desiring production which, as they point out, are bound by introjection and projection.

In the specialised literature, life in contexts of extreme urban poverty is often described in terms of lack and need; the conditions and variables used in such descriptions serve to compare, analyse and assess the seriousness of the different situations in relation to what is lacking. Clearly in keeping with the processes of impoverishment that characterised the 1990s, in recent years different scales (the poverty line and unmet basic needs[5] are the two most common, though there are others) and categorisations of poverty (the poor, the new poor, population at risk, socially vulnerable children, indigence, etc.) have been developed in an attempt to produce increasingly precise measures of unmet needs. In a certain way, then, these categorisations serve to differentiate shades of grey, so to speak, only relevant to statistical or sociological debates but that, in the real lives of people, are largely irrelevant and frivolous. Indeed, to what extent can such dramatic and virulent unmet needs be rendered and isolated by social measurement, risk indices and/or statistics?

Such conceptualisations are in keeping with the images we see on the television,[6] where youth and poverty are either criminalised or seen as a horror show.[7] The mass media images of poor neighbourhoods entail two visions that are, in fact, two sides of the same coin. On the one hand, disease, crime and/or drugs and, on the other, situations where, due to great power of will, someone manages to escape these contexts. One is either criminal and, hence, destined to live there, or a hero who manages to get out.[8] In both cases, the neighbourhood is represented as an infected place, one that must not be entered or must be left behind. As we will discuss later, the media images of these places tend to coincide with the teachers' descriptions.[9] What they have to say about the students is not much better: they often mention pregnant teenagers who don't know how to take care of their babies. Of course, being pregnant is 'prohibited' to these young women, and if they are mothers they don't know how to take care of their children. The young people who live in these neighbourhoods are often described as drug addicts and pregnant girls. The desiring production of the people who live there, the way they actually live, is nowhere to be found in any possible imagination, narrative or display. But these are the very concerns of these young women when they pick up the camera. To use the words of Deleuze and Guattari, 'the administration of a great organised molar security has as its correlate a whole micro-management of petty fears, a permanent molecular insecurity ... a macropolitics of society by and for a micropolitics of insecurity' (2000, 220).

Returning to the idea of the abject, we ask ourselves, along with Butler (2002), what opposition and/or resistance can the sphere of the excluded and the abject enact against the hegemony that determines which bodies and lifestyles matter, which ones are worth protecting, saving and/or bemoaning their losses? What do these young women who live in these excluded and abject territories have to say, what do they show, what stance do they take?

Given the characteristics of the processes we are witnessing and studying, I think we can observe how, in a very particular way, school life combines situations that, though totally commonplace, fully expose both the extreme nature of the lives and the desiring-production of these young people. In other words, the students with their camera fully expose a traumatised territory and certain living conditions. But in and around those conditions, these students show the image of children at play, rather than the image of crime. That is, to return to Nietzsche and Deleuze the image of the will to live, of desiring production, production that resoundingly affirms the unit that not only expresses lacks that must be filled but that also produces the real (Deleuze and Guattari 1995).

Therefore, we are speaking of the life of subjects, the dynamics of school life in terms of these young women and their production: a video documentary that expresses their interests, concerns, desires, aspirations ... Hence, below I will focus specifically on the video and its contents.

The documentary video: everyday banality

In the workshop and the video, these young women offer another vision of shantytowns, one that differs from those that only display crime, death and laziness. While this vision has many forms and nuances, it always expresses the recognition of the neighbourhood as a place of their own, a place of life, a place of friendship. I want to underline the sense of affirmation that is constantly felt when these young women speak of their lives. For instance, in the following dialogue about the place they live:

> Nair: No, the thing is I am a little sad...
> Interviewer: Why are you sad?
> N: Well, I have my reasons.
> I: Do you want to tell me about it...?
> N: Well, it looks like I have to move to Moreno.[10]
> ...
> And I don't want to go ... my friends are here... (Nair, a 13-year-old girl, documentary video, from here on referred to as DV)

Carcova[11] is where Nair was born, where she, her friends and her family live; it's her place, and so she doesn't want to leave it, but rather live there as best she can, as we all do. That does not mean that Nair and her peers do not see or speak of the problems in the neighbourhood. But they don't want to move out of it; they want, rather, to improve it. Indeed, the video is about trash, and that is not a coincidence. As the video reveals, from a variety of perspectives trash is one of the most serious problems in these extremely diminished and degraded urban spaces (Davies 2008), whether because the families look for food in the land fields; because they gather and live from the trash that they collect and sell; or because the trash surrounds them in an urban space where there is no trash collection service. The choice of the topic, the spaces and the narratives filmed are political statements, but those statements are never made on the basis of negation but rather of desiring affirmation. Thus, Nair says in the video:

> I hope that this project shows people that Carcova is just another place, like any other; the difference is money but money can't buy love... (DV)

And this, I think, is what the video narrates. It is the everyday situations, the most banal scenes (Deleuze 2005) – a kid with a balloon, a boy riding a tricycle, girls playing with dolls – that express the extremity of the situation, and that is because in these conditions there is desire, there is life. As the students say in the video, this is where we live; there is life here, there are people; it's not just a trash dump like people think. In speaking about the video, Nair says:

> It's good because we are showing what there is in Carcova, we are showing something ... something hidden that no one, no government has ever paid attention to ... and that's awful because for people with money it's like Carcova doesn't exist, it's like a trash dump where we live and that's not true... (Nair, DV)

I believe that this student makes a crucial point here. The camera shows a polluted *zanjon* (a local term for a sort of drainage stream) full of trash. Nair is one of the students who suggested that the video be about trash. She didn't want to show only a trash dump, though. She wanted to show the place where she lives. It's not only a question of meeting needs or satisfying lack; but that does not imply that these needs do not exist. They do and they are many, but what defines the neighbourhood, what these young people want to show, is precisely that there is life here as well. Nair goes on to say:

> ...this is where we grow up. There are people, there are kids, there is friendship, there is life, there are flowers, there are fights, there is definitely love because fights are very romantic ... Daniela has a boyfriend, right Daniela?
>
> Daniela: Fights are romantic.
> Nair: Life is romantic.
> (Laughter)
> Last spring filled us with love...' (Nair and Daniela, 12 years old, DV)

This dialogue between Nair and Daniela deals with a number of questions. First, they do not deny the conditions in which they live; in fact, they want to show them, make them visible. They say that that is something hidden, perhaps even abject. But television shows also feature shantytowns. What's special about this act of showing, this appearing? Nair and Daniela are speaking of life, of their desires. Where the television shows crime, they want to show something other than a trash dump, they want to show that there is love here, that Daniela has a boyfriend. Returning to Deleuze, what we find here is not need but desire. But desires are produced and shift in certain conditions.

These are banal, simple, everyday situations, yet ones laden with meaning. In the words of Deleuze,

> If everyday banality is so important it is because, being subject to sensory-motor schemata which are automatic and pre-established, it is all the more liable, on the least disturbance of equilibrium between stimulus and response, suddenly to free itself of the laws of this schema and reveal itself in a visual and sound nakedness, crudeness and brutality which make it unbearable, giving it the pace of a dream or a nightmare. (Deleuze 2005, 18)

Pages later, Deleuze says that the distinctions between the trivial and the extreme, or between the real and the imaginary, or between the objective and the subjective are relative, and that's because there is constant passage between those apparently polar terms: accumulated dead forces emitted by the most trivial situations.

The *zanjon* is one of the many drainage creeks in Greater Buenos Aires, where the city's sewers and industrial waste is drained. In the shantytown, the organised channel comes to an end, and turns into an open creek: when it reaches the neighbourhood, the creek brings in all the city's waste; it is also where the neighbourhood's pit latrines drain and where, since there is no public sanitation service, many people throw their own trash. To keep the trash from piling too high, people often burn it, leading to a third form of pollution: smoke. In the students' narrative and in the images that they film of the creek, we see trash as well as children playing.

This is probably one of the most tragic images/statements in the film: it is where the trivial becomes the extreme. Here, where pollution does not seem to let anything live, here where all there seems to be is smoke, dirty and polluted water, open sewers, trash and waste, this is where we find children playing. This image, not the one shown on TV, is the crudest. The television shows poverty as spectacle, a spectacle of drugs, violence, theft and ruined lives. In a situation as banal as children playing hide and seek or a girl pretending to be a motorcycle rider, we are faced with a naked image, with the extreme, with what we don't want to see: mainly, people living. There is nothing more intimidating than the confirmation of life when all we expect is death. Because abject fear turns these places into unliveable zones full of people that the Greeks would have, in an instant, called *animal laborans*. But, in this everyday banality, these young women simply show, as Arendt would say, the human condition that, in these spaces, is systematically denied and rejected (Figures 1 and 2).

Poverty, even extreme poverty, has become bearable. What's not, though, is what we see in these images, the ones I don't know whether to call dreamlike or nightmarish: the image, for instance, of young people playing amidst the smoke. Perhaps that is the statement of resistance: where, in the midst of the trivial, the extreme emerges. Rather than lack, we find statements of affirmation, statements of desire (see Ringrose 2010) (Figure 3).

When the adults who work with these young people every day saw the video, their desiring production is what had the greatest impact on them. The teachers thanked us for showing them another image of their students.

What, then, is this other image?

Although the students at the school come from various 'greys' of poverty, the ones that made this video are, according to the teachers, from the 'worst' group.[12] As stated before, the teachers are constantly complaining that they cannot work with these kids, that they are vandals, that they climb the walls, that they are drug addicts, girls with unwanted pregnancies, that they cut wire fences. Of course, these vandals are sometimes *poor little things* because their parents are in jail, or they have to take care of their brothers and sisters, and so forth…

Figure 1. Playing hide and seek in the Zanjon.

Figure 2. Girl pretending to be a motorcycle rider.

These vandals were the ones who produced this video. And that's what is shocking: to find these students doing, producing, thinking and saying. Another crucial element in the video is, I think, the tension that characterises school life and, especially, the relationship between young people and teachers. Because, on the one hand, the video shows images of poverty and marginality that question any possibility for

Figure 3. Young people playing amidst the smoke.

education and, on the other, it constantly manifests that, before a sustained proposal, all the young people do is show interest and the desire to participate. The first of those terms entails a negation of any possibility of learning and, hence, is evidence of the purposelessness of teaching. That, of course, makes it impossible to understand why these young people, who supposedly can no longer take an interest in anything, keep going to school. As the principal of the school said when we started working together:

> You see that student over there? We told him not to come to school today because his teachers were absent, and look, here he is.

The students go to school anyway, even when there are no classes or when they know they have to repeat the year. It's common to see them at the corner, waiting to go inside. The school is still a meeting place where students go in the hopes of finding something that might interest them. Families keep seeing schools as the best place for their children to be. Upon seeing the video that her daughter had made, one mother, moved and surprised, said to me, 'I am very pleased with what she is doing'.

Schools do not always manage to produce these spaces. Indeed, many of the situations that take place every day in classrooms and schoolyards produce just the opposite. To refer to Deleuze and Guattari once again 'Desire, then, becomes the abject fear of lacking something. But it should be noted that this is not a phrase uttered by the poor or dispossessed' (1995, 34). I think something of that is what happens in schools every day. It is also expressed in the video in an interview that the students do in a street adjacent to the shantytown. This scene includes an older woman (the grandmother) and a 10-year-old child (the grandson), at the door to their home, and the students with the camera, who are asking them what they know about the shantytown and the *zanjon*. This is the conversation:

> Students: What do you know about the *zanjon*?
> Neighbour: Nothing…

S:	About trash burning?
N:	Nothing.
S:	About Carcova?
N:	Not a thing.
(Student to the grandchild):	None of your classmates live in Carcova?
N:	No, he doesn't go to that school…
Grandson:	But one kid at school lives in the shantytown.
N:	Who?
G:	Franco.
N:	OK … just one… (interview by DV students)

Thus, what is hidden is where we don't want to end up. More than hidden, it is the object of abject fear, a fear that is more patent the closer you are to the *zanjon*, and more jarring when you live very near where the channel turns into the creek. Deleuze and Guattari go on: 'This involves deliberately organising wants and needs amid an abundance of production, making all of desire teeter and fall victim of the great fear of not having one's need satisfied' (1995, 35). Fear of not having one's needs satisfied in a world in which we are all at risk, in the self-declared risk society, becomes fear of even being near these spaces. Abject fear is the other side of a narcissist society.

For those who live in these abject spaces, for those who were born there, for those whose parents and, in many cases, grandparents were born there, that fear does not exist. What exists is life in those spaces and the desire that shifts in those conditions and, most certainly, utterances produced in that space. Utterances whose clarity is patent; there is nothing to interpret, nothing to analyse … The *zanjon*, the trash, the burning of the trash and children playing hide and seek. Nothing to hide, nothing to analyse…

The affirmation produced in the video is by no means a negation of the living conditions in the neighbourhood. For Nair, once again, those conditions are a reality, something that happens when there is no alternative. In the following dialogue, Nair argues with one of her classmates who laughs at the people who, like some of the young people or family members of the young women who made this video, go to rummage for food in the CEAMSE:[13]

Nair:	…I am telling you. Let's hope that never in your life you have to come here … because you come off real bad saying everything you are saying … real bad…
Nilson:	I am saying that no matter what happens am I not going to stoop to that.
N:	One day, your parents are going to lose their jobs or, God forbid, they are going to die and you are going to have to come here… (dialogue between Nair and Nilson, a classmate, DV)

This dialogue can be read in a number of ways, but I am interested in pointing out two things. First, the *let's hope* with which Nair begins her sentence. She is not saying it's OK that people live this way, or glorifying a situation so cruel that it leads a group of people to search for food in a trash dump. There is no romanticism here. But there is – and this is my second point – an account of the living conditions of the thousands who, every day in these global times, lose their jobs. And that most certainly involves the reproduction of individuals and families as well as the reality of the territories in which they live. This often means not only losing one's job but receiving a salary that is only enough to pay for a place to live. As the father of one of the teenagers says:

We lived in Munro but what I earned was only enough to pay for the room we lived in…

Thus, the video is also a clear and resounding testimony of inequality and social injustice. A testimony that becomes more beautiful – if that word can be used to speak of these situations – at the moment that the vision of these young people shows poverty not only as an expression of growing and traumatic social injustice, but, and more importantly, as the human condition in various senses. Where all we see is criminals, they show life, they show that life is produced; they reveal the social nature of the forgetting and of the denial of history that our societies produce every day.

In brief, they show us the abject as something formed and produced by history in certain social relations. In the words of Yamila:

> Interviewer: What are some things you like?
> Y: I like everything ... I like playing with my friends ... when we went to CEAMSE ... that was good ... because we saw all sorts of things there ... I had already been there ... but anyway ...No ... the guy from CEAMSE was good ... He spoke of things that *you*[14] care about ... I didn't enjoy it ... but I didn't mind what he was saying, what he said was true ... but it would be bad if ... if they closed it, right? If they close it people are not going to have anything to eat ... people who don't have work. (Yamila, 13 years old, DV)

Next, and I think this is crucial, by means of the video the young women hope for something; they hope that someone sees it; they hope that someone listens to them; they hope to show and appear in a greater social scene that systematically denies, rejects and expulses them.

And so when we say that young people are nihilistic, that they don't care about anything, I immediately remember Agamben's words:

> There has never been a more revolting sight than that of a generation of adults which having destroyed all remaining possibilities of authentic experience lays its own impoverishment at the door of a younger generation bereft of the capacity for experience. When mankind is deprived of effective experience and becomes subjected to the imposition of a form of experience as controlled and manipulated as a laboratory maze for rats – in other words, when the only possible experience is horror and lies – then the rejection of experience can provisionally embody a legitimate defense. (2001, 12)

Perhaps that is the lesson learned. And, addressing the adults who work in the schools, I would like them to understand that nihilism does not come from young people.

Closing notes

On the basis of field work at schools in contexts of extreme urban poverty, in this paper I have ventured to offer a way to see and conceive young people in general and these teenage women in particular. What begins to emerge here is something that lies beyond nihilism, violence and apathy. Far from the images in the mass media and the obligatory articles about teens in the specialised literature, we have, in this project and with these teens, come across ways of being that are connected to life, to desire. I believe that such production is a political reading of their own living conditions, that is, the living conditions in those unliveable spaces like the poorest neighbourhoods in Argentina and the rest of Latin America. Thus, the way these teenagers tell their stories evidences the contradictions and tensions that mark their lives while heeding the place of school and adults; this video shows, that is, processes of subjectivation and desiring production. I have attempted to emphasise and expose the complexity of these processes, productions and subjects by offering a detailed analysis of multiple discourses, as well as their intersections and contradictions (Youdell 2006). This is crucial to grasping the details of the multiple fragments and contrasts that characterise a traumatised daily life.

Thus, in these contexts of social trauma, we ask ourselves to what extent the image of the paralysed subject of that trauma (Ankersmit 2008) is not interdicted in the doing of these young people. Returning to the notion of the abject, I propose, along with Deleuze and Guattari, that in these urban contexts there is no place for abject fear; indeed, its underside is presented in the work of these young people. Thus, I propose, in keeping with Deleuze (2005), that it is in the trivial, in the most banal and everyday reality that these situations become extreme and even explicit affirmations of life, ways out. Both in the choice of topic and in the students' opinions thereof, this production constitutes a political statement. Indeed, those traumatic and traumatising situations become simple images of what lies in these contexts. As Ankersmit points out, all this takes place in the double condition of the traumatic yet sublime experience of the world: this is where the experience becomes immediate. Indeed, these young women do not hesitate to position themselves in this immediateness or to show it through the camera. Where one expects to see death, these young women attest to life. I believe that constitutes an image of resistance in a number of senses: the resistance of life itself and the testimony of those who, despite the worst possible conditions, produce, live, desire. Resistance as a way out that does not refer to the death and/or disappearance of the subject, to subjects with no interests, or to dangerous youth, but, rather resistance that shows youth expressing and affirming its concerns, emotions and interests. A resistance that renders the abject full of life, that is, fills with life that which constitutes, in my view, the core of abject fear, which is often experienced as a threat to good urban consciences.

We wonder, in times where it would seem that rebellion is no longer possible (Kristeva 1999), at times when the absence and impossibility of experience has been decreed, if the production of these young women might constitute *sui generis* forms of resistance, that is, moment-images of unrest. In a world where the will to nothing reigns, a world of abjection, the affirmation of life constitutes, perhaps, an act of resistance.

This differs from the image of resistance that Willis so aptly describes in *Learning to Labour*, where the culture clash led to dropping out of school. These students do not drop out; they insist, they stick with it. It is not, for them, a question of leaving a place but staying there, improving it and also making trouble. Indeed, this very making-of-trouble is often experienced as a threat by adults, especially at school. This is even more the case when teens strive to show that they are good, that they study, that they work ... as the students often say, for instance, 'we're from the hood but we're good'. At school, the characterisation of these young women goes from maladjusted vandals to poor little things incapable of doing anything. In that space, a space doubly untenable for any educational undertaking, we find young people who stand up and speak, who keep going to school.

I have attempted to show, in keeping with Ringrose (2010), the multiple forms of these young women's gaze, how their words render them political subjects even in contexts like these where their very citizenship is denied. This becomes a threat when they narrate their lives or when their lives start to matter. In other words, I understand the source of discomfort and disturbance, and the act of resistance, to take place when these girls move out of the two places expected of them, the place of the criminal or the victim, by expressing, producing and affirming their difference. If as Deleuze and Guattari state, 'desire does not lack anything. It is, rather, the subject that is missing in desire' (1995, 33), we ask ourselves who the nihilists really are.

Notes
1. I am referring to several incidents that took place in middle schools in Argentina that received a great deal of public attention, for instance a video on YouTube where students burned a teacher's hair.
2. While it might be interesting to discuss the dynamics of the workshop itself, that exceeds the scope of this article.
3. In 1978, during the military dictatorship, the decree numbers 21,809 and 21,810, which transferred control of grade schools to the provincial states were passed; and in 1992, Congress passed Law Ley 24,049 which effected the transferal of control of high schools and post-high school institutions. In neither case were the funds that would enable the provinces to handle the tasks allocated by the national government. These processes constitute a clear example of neo-liberal educational policies in Latin America in general and Argentina in particular (see, among others, Sader and Gentili 2001).
4. If that might seem obvious, it ceases to be so when, to take an example from educational policy, governmental documents and policies ponder what can be done in schools despite poverty, as if poverty were a variable that could be isolated.
5. The 'poverty line' measures whether a home's income can meet a set of basic nutritional and non-nutritional needs (clothing, education, health care, etc.) included in what is called the *Canasta Básica Total* (CBT). *Población con Necesidades Básicas Insatisfechas* (NBI) refers to that population characterised by one of the following: more than three people living in a room; inhabiting precarious dwellings or tenements that lack toilets with running water; any child of school age (6–12 years) who does not attend school.
6. Although there are differences between the television shows that depict the criminalisation of poverty, we are speaking particularly of news programmes where the images of shantytowns are associated with crime, drug addiction and/or pregnant teens (see, among others, Saintout 2002)
7. One such programme is *Policías en acción* (Police in Action) that shows actual police operatives.
8. Though it deals with another Third World country, the film *Slumdog Millionaire* entails the image of someone who strives to get out.
9. We are speaking about statements made in informal conversations where the teachers complain about the students and the impossibility of working with them as well as their descriptions of the students in more formal and in-depth interviews carried out as part of the research.
10. Moreno is another town in Greater Buenos Aires. To go from Carcova to Moreno, you must take several buses.
11. Carcova, the name of the shantytown where these kids live, is also the name of a very important Argentine painter. One of his famous paintings, *Sin pan y sin trabajo* (*Without Bread and Without Work*, 1892) deals with the working class and its life in the then-incipient shantytowns.
12. This is the term that the teachers used to describes these young women at the beginning of the workshop. Due to limitations of space, here we only make brief reference to these characterisations in order to provide for better understanding of the dynamics of the workshop and what these young women propose in their video.
13. CEAMSE ('Coordinación Ecológica Área Metropolitana Sociedad Del Estado') is the leading company in waste transport and disposal, with more than 31 years of experience in this field. Here, the students are referring to the land field where much of the trash produced in the city of Buenos Aires is deposited. Many families go to these land fields looking for food every day.
14. Yamila uses the pronoun *you* when she seems to be speaking of herself. Two lines later, she does the same thing when speaking of people who are not going to have anything to eat. As with many other families, such people are her grandmother, her uncle, her mother, etc.

References

Agamben, G. 1998. *Homo sacer. El poder soberano y la nuda vida.* Valencia: Pre-textos.
Ankersmit, F. 2008. *Experiencia histórica sublime.* Santiago, Chile: Palinodia.
Araya Gomez, Gabriela. 2003. Etnografía audiovisual y escrita: Una reflexión desde la Antropología Feminista. *Revista Austral de Ciencias Sociales* 2003, no. 7: 153–64.
Ardévol, E. 1998. Por una antropología de la mirada: Etnografía, epresentación y construcción de datos audiovisuales. Revista de Dialectologia y Tradiciones Populares del CSIC, Perspectivas de la Antropologia Visual, Madrid.
Bell, V. 2007. *Culture & performance.* Oxford: Berg.
Britzman, D. 1992. Decentering discourse in teacher education: or the unleashing of unpopular things. In *What can school do?,* ed. K. Weiler and C. Mitchell, 151–72. Buffalo: State University of New York.
Butler, J. 2002. *Cuerpos que importan. Sobre los límites materiales y discursivos del 'sexo'.* Buenos Aires: Paidós.
Davies, M. 2008. *Planeta de ciudades miseria.* Madrid: Foca.
de Certeau, M. 2007. *La invención de lo cotidiano.* Madrid: UIA.
Deleuze, G. 2005. *La imagen-movimento.* Buenos Aires: Paidós.
Deleuze, G., and F. Guattari. 1995. *El antiedipo. Capitalismo y esquizofrenia.* Buenos Aires: Paidós.
Deleuze, G., and F. Guattari. 2000. *Mil mesetas.* Valencia: Pre-textos.
Foucault, M. 2006. *Seguridad territorio y población.* Argentina: Fondo de Cultura Económica.
Foucault, M. 2007. *El nacimiento de la biopolítica.* Argentina: Fondo de Cultura Económica.
Grinberg, S. 2008. *Educación y poder en el siglo XXI.* Buenos Aires, Argentina: Miño y Dávila Editores.
Kristeva, J. 1988. *Poderes de la perversión.* Catálogus, Siglo XXI, Argentina.
Kristeva, J. 1999. *Sentido y sinsentido de la rebeldía.* Chile: Editorial Cuarto Propio.
McNay, Lois. 1992. *Foucault and feminism: Power, gender and the self.* Cambridge: Polity Press.
Pink, S. 2008. Mobilising visual ethnography: Making routes, making place and making images. *Forum: qualitative social research* 9, no. 3, art. 36, September 2008. http://www.qualitative-research.net/fqs/.
O'Malley, P. 2007. Experimentos en gobierno. Analíticas gubernamentales y conocimiento estratégico del riesgo. In *Revista Argentina de Sociología.* Argentina: Miño y Dávila editors.
Ringrose, J. 2010. Beyond Discourse? Using Deleuze and Guattari's schizoanalysis to explore affective assemblages, heterosexually striated space, and lines of flight online and at school. *Educational Philosophy and Theory.* DOI: 10.1111/j.1469-5812.2009.00601.x.
Rose, N., 1999. *Powers of freedom. Reframing political thought.* Cambridge, UK: Cambridge University Press.
Rose, N., P. O'Malley, and M. Valverde. 2006. Governmentality. *Law & Society, Annual Review* 2: 83.
Sader, E., and P. Gentili. 2001. *Las tramas del neoliberalismo.* Buenos Aires: Eudeba.
Saintout, F. 2002. La criminalizaicón de los jóvenes en la TV: los pibes chorros. *Signo y Pensamiento* (Universidad Javeriana, Bogotá), no. 41, July/December.
Willis, P. 1998. *Aprendiendo a trabajar.* Madrid: España Akal.
Youdell, D. 2006. *Impossible bodies, impossible selves: Exclusion and student subjectivities.* Dordrecht: Springer.

Charting cartographies of resistance: lines of flight in women artists' narratives

Maria Tamboukou

Centre for Narrative Research, University of East London, Docklands Campus, University Way, London E16 2RD, UK

> In this paper I chart lines of flight in women artist's narratives. In focusing on the complex interrelations between the social milieus of education and art, what I suggest is that they should be analysed as an *assemblage* where power relations and forces of desire are constantly at play in creating conditions of possibility for women to resist, imagine themselves becoming other and for new possibilities in their lives to be actualised. As a novel approach to social ontology the theory of assemblages offers an analytics of social complexity that accounts for open configurations, continuous connections and unstable hierarchies, structures and axes of difference. In reconsidering resistance as immanent in *dispositifs* of power and *assemblages* of desire, what I finally argue is that women artists' narratives contribute to the constitution of minor knowledges and create archives of radical futurity.

> I got a grant and I went to Art School feeling very peculiar because ... nobody went to Art School ... being working class, you had to earn a living and artists don't earn a living, do they? ... And a woman artist was almost sort of in the same way that they thought about actresses ... that's the next step on to, you know, prostitution or something ghastly like that. (Interview with Irene Runayker, 3 March 2006)

Irene Runayker[1] grew up during the Second World War as a working-class girl in West Ham, East London and studied art at the Camberwell School of Arts and Crafts and at the Central School of Art. She has painted and exhibited widely while at the same time working as an art teacher in various schools of the Inner London Educational Authority. Notwithstanding the difficulties emerging from her working-class background, Runayker did study art right after school. However, the harsh reality of having to support herself, while striving to become an artist, had a huge effect on how her career unfolded:

> I wasn't really eating very well and got quite ill and went to see the doctor ... and he gave me thorough examinations, he said actually 'you are very anaemic and I am going to give you some iron tablets and you take three a day you are quite undernourished, after a meal and I said, 'well, can I take the three of them after one meal' and he said 'no you can't, why you ask?' And I said 'well I only eat once a day' ... a lot of us were like that we didn't have any money, it was incredible ... Anyway so there I was, I was 20 years old, I got married and had to go out to work and had to stand on my feet again and I had

> my first son when I was 22 and was doing a little painting but nothing very ... there was no continuum. I had my second ... we moved from Hampstead, and I had my second son in 1966 by which time I had started teaching for an inner London educational authority, teaching infants in King's Cross ... became Deputy Head and in five years, six years Deputy headship and 15 months at the Headship ... by which time the marriage had broken up and I just had to put in as much work as I could to get as much money as I could. (Interview with Irene Runayker, 3 March 2006)

As is boldly articulated in Runayker's narrative, life intervened after the carefree years of the Art School and that had a decisive impact on her career as an artist. Runayker's story thus forcefully expresses the difficulties that women in general and women artists in particular face within the constraints and limitations of juggling with multifarious tasks: doing art, having a family and working to make ends meet, ultimately leading interrupted lives. In her narrative, Runayker emphasises the fact that interruptions and delays were particularly considered as detrimental for an artist's career.

> This was another barrier that unless you started early and got known early and therefore you made all your connections early and your name was known, then forget about it. That was one of the myths. Forget about it. So I had this feeling when, you know, that I was going to miss out on everything again, because I missed out from it because I did marry young ... I had the children and then that meant 14 years more or less out of my practice, so I thought I'd missed the boat and I am a woman and I am a working-class woman, so there were all of these things: you shouldn't have got married and you should have got married well and you should have got somebody to look after you ... Instead taking the route that I did take. (Interview with Irene Runayker, 3 March 2006)

And yet, Runayker's story shows that life can always go beyond the restraints of discourses and myths – this is actually, the beauty of life: emerging possibilities of transgression as expressed in the narrative below.

> I knew that this was the wrong road for me I didn't want even for survival sake, I did not want to keep doing this ... I really had to go back and do some painting again and really, the terrible worry was I wouldn't be able to earn enough money teaching in order to keep my family ... By this time I was at the top salary of the grades that I was on and so I thought, well, actually I could do this and I will give it five years so I left, got a part-time job teaching, two and a half, three days a week in a local school and started painting again. (Interview with Irene Runayker, 3 March 2006)

Starting painting again was indeed a difficult but necessary decision in Runayker's life, but it became even harsher by the initial fear that she might have had irretrievably missed the train. However, it was actually life's pains and torments that were filling her canvases with beautiful images and forms and were unleashing aesthetic forces and lines of flight.[2]

> So I started again in 1975 and that first year's painting was horrendous, I mean, I cannot tell you how bad they were, it was as if I never had any training at all, but suddenly round, round at about the end of that year, beginning of 75, 76, suddenly everything dropped, all the pennies began to drop and I started painting stuff that I know all those years before I wouldn't be able to do. It was almost as if life itself, the living of it had enabled me to express myself in paint, and I cannot understand, I couldn't sort of, I can't explain how this came about but I know that this is true, that there is something to do, this link up with life and with art, that there is something to do being involved with people and with your society or with your family whoever, but being involved in some way feeds back into the richness of what happens on your canvas and this has been this

has come up time and time again that … both liberates you on the canvas or in your work and, and … and you also find a way of expressing it. OK, so we've got there. (Interview with Irene Runayker, 3 March 2006)

I started this paper with a forceful narrative: a working-class woman telling her story of becoming an artist. Runayker's story emerged in the context of an AHRC-funded project entitled 'In the Fold Between Life and Art, a Genealogy of Women Artists'.[3] In this project I have explored interfaces between life and art in auto/biographical narratives and paintings of women artists. Drawing on Foucauldian and DeleuzoGuattarian analytics, I have been interested in the interrelation of ethics, aesthetics and politics in the constitution of the female self in art. In this light I have traced women artists' nomadic paths as they make their life a work of art, in the process of resisting what they are, becoming other. Being a genealogy, the archive of my research has included a wide range of published and unpublished auto/biographical narratives from the turn of the nineteenth century as well as contemporary life history interviews.[4] These narratives have been explored as effects of power relations and forces of desire but also as sites for the constitution of the real and the subject herself.[5] In this light I have challenged an image of narratives as unified and coherent representations of lives and subjects, but have also pointed to their importance in opening up microsociological analyses of deterritorialisations and lines of flight.[6]

Runayker's powerful storyline above that 'life itself, the living of it had enabled me to express myself in paint' seemed to emerge from a diagram of multifarious connections between life and art, the initial idea of my genealogy; it was a rich life-history interview, not however because it responded to my research hypothesis. One could always argue that my research hypothesis had somehow elicited, or at least effectuated the kind of narrative I had got and there is indeed rich literature in narrative research around it.[7] Having for years interrogated and problematised 'the spontaneity' and unproblematic referentiality of narratives, I was not so much excited about the confirmation of my hypothesis. What has really intrigued me in this narrative is something that I had not initially thought of in designing my research: the forceful network of relations between education and art particularly saturated by the impact of social class upon women artists' lives.

In previous research on women teachers' auto/biographical narratives[8] I have theorised art as a heterotopic field sheltering women teachers in crisis and opening up spaces of creativity and escape from the sometimes-unbearable heaviness of teaching. Indeed, women teachers' attachment to art was a theme very frequently traced in their self-writings. What had intrigued me most in these narratives is that women teachers' passionate interest in art was not simply a matter of passive admiration of artistic objects; it was closely interrelated to ways of living, practices through which they have actively constituted themselves as subjects, by deploying what I have theorised, drawing on Foucault (1988), as *technologies of the female self*.[9]

The strong emotions and affects expressed in women teachers' narratives about the works of arts in the galleries they visited, the theatrical plays and the concerts they attended, and the literary creation they were often involved in, stirred their passion to live a beautiful, but also unconventional life and influenced their choices, beliefs and life attitudes. Being under the spell of the various *fin-de-siècle* artistic movements, women teachers' lives seemed to transgress class boundaries. Working-class teacher Mary Smith would admit that 'poetry indeed was through all the hard periods of my life, my joy and strength, the uplifter of my soul in trouble' (1892, 242).

Dina Copelman has further shown that although elementary women teachers in London did not have the means to take full advantage of London's cultural events, they did enjoy a greater choice of activities and 'participated in the culture – the places, spaces, events and services – that was being created to cater to New Women' (1996, 167). In this context, Molly Vivian Hughes was excited at the idea of taking the omnibus to go to the theatre, instead of 'being taken' and did not mind having to wait in queues for a good seat in the gallery, or having to bear bad lighting and inadequate ventilation, since 'all the discomforts were forgotten as soon as the curtain went up' (1996, 169). Hughes' experience was shared by many other women teachers who according to Copelman, 'more than indulging a personal infatuation or a love of the theatre ... were participating in an exploration of the boundaries of contemporary femininity' (1996, 169). The Poplars Dramatic Society, for example, was according to Copelman (1985, 209) composed mostly of male and female teachers. Helen Corke, a young teacher from the labour aristocracy, would depict her passionate life search for beauty in her autobiographical novel *Neutral Ground*, while recounting her return to her South London home, after a moving performance:

> from each twinkling sky sign, and each electric moon that swung luminous over Piccadilly and Buckingham Palace Road ... echoed the radiant ecstasy of the Fire music. It sang from the big trains pulsing over the river, and even from the dark river itself. London was beautiful. Why had she never noticed its beauty before? (cited in Copelman 1996, 170)

Women teachers' aesthetic orientations and passion for art would sometimes lead them to abandon teaching for good, as with Cicely Hamilton, who eventually followed a career as an actress; for others art would offer a break from the stress of teaching life, as was the case with the Girtonian pioneer and founder of Westfield College, Constance Maynard:

> This third year at St. Andrews was to me even more strangling and choking than before. *I wanted to tear it right in half and get out, out into air and freedom and to be myself.* All through my life I have been an artist manqué and there was a lion within that raged and roared at times. (emphasis added)[10]

In the above extract Constance Maynard powerfully expresses her drive to get away from St. Andrews, where she had worked for three years as a teacher, just after her graduation from Girton College. Having realised her life dream of getting an education, the enthusiastic Girtonian pioneer was feeling trapped and suffocated within the educational institutions she had fought so hard to enter. In escaping teaching she turned to art and for two years she attended the famous Slade School of Fine Art in London:

> So I toiled through the loneliness of Cheltenham and the extreme tension and trial of the three years at St. Andrews, which left me with a pervading sense of failure. I had tried my very best and had failed. Then came the sudden bursting of bonds, the leaving my miseries behind in the orange-coloured sunset sky that glowed and the plunge into the entire freedom and happiness of my two Sessions at the School of Art. The first Slade School year seems to me as I look back of it to be unclouded, with its hours of silent and successful work, its warm friendships ... and its magnificent whole-hearted meetings of several different kinds.[11]

In the context of my previous research then with women teachers' narratives, art was configured as an alternative real and imaginary space, somewhere to create, but also to retreat, reflect and reinvent the self. My current research of writing a genealogy of women artists (Tamboukou 2010) has actually unveiled the dark side of the moon. While some women teachers have leaped into the world of art in an attempt to escape the boredom and frustration of their working lives, women artists have found in education a place to shelter themselves, as they are striving in the harsh realities of the artworld. There is a whole history around this reverse movement, to which I now turn.

Women have been historically excluded from education in general and art education in particular. Education, however, has been also the locus where counter-discourses and counter-practices emerged, to oppose the truth regimes, cultural conditions and social structures that had legitimated and perpetuated women's exclusion. Education is thus a site where juxtaposing discourses are framing women's lives, but still a theatre of local struggles and resistance, a transitional space in these lives. In this light, the movement for the higher education of women has had a tremendous impact on reshaping women's private and public lives as well as shattering the discursive boundaries between the very distinction between the private and the public.

While however the turn of the nineteenth century marked a significant shift in women's educational opportunities, art education has remained an exclusionary field at least for working-class women for much longer. There was a reason for it, beautifully articulated in Runayker's narrative: 'nobody went to Art School because you know, being working class, you had to earn a living and artists don't earn a living, do they?'

The rationale for women's inclusion in all levels of education has been historically founded on the argument that women had to work; it was an argument revolving around the Protestant ethic of the importance of work and the evil of idleness. Art education was therefore by definition a grey area, since it could not possibly be linked to the prospective of a profession or of real work, particularly so, for working-class women. Middle-class women as well would stay away from Art Education, since it carried the risk of detracting them once again from the world of professions they were striving to enter. As Penny Dalton has noted: 'Discourses of the "lady artist" have proliferated in the modern period and are continually being reactivated. The ideology of the 'lady amateur' has been synonymous with bad art; art that is unprofessional, weak, unskilled, trivial, bourgeois, merely decorative' (2001, 47).

Of course women artists at the turn of the century did work hard to establish a professional identity and historical studies have shown that becoming a professional artist was a prospect for some women of the middle classes.[12] Anne Brontë's heroine in the *Tenant of Wildfell Hall* has influentially reflected that possibility in the world of literature. Things were very different for working-class women however. It goes without saying that art education became available for working-class people in general and working-class women in particular in the late part of the nineteenth century. However, the kind of art education to which the masses could have access was far away from the idea of Classical Art. As Dalton's (2001) study has shown, in the context of the nineteenth century art education was deployed as a gendered discourse and was deeply shaped by the needs of industrial modernisation. Art education was therefore both classed and gendered and this historical legacy has lived up to our own days.

What my research has also unearthed is that art education has not only been perceived as an irrelevant field for working-class people, but also an immoral one for women in general and working-class women in particular. This point is succinctly noted in Runayker's narrative above: 'and a woman artist was almost sort of in the same way that they thought about actresses ... that's the next step on to, you know, prostitution or something ghastly like that'. Her narrative reverberates with Pauline Crook's story of becoming an artist:

> Well I was born in 51 so and I left school at 16 which would have been in 1968 and I just come from very much a working-class family and I wanted to go to art college ... but in those days you couldn't get a grant until you were about 18 and my parents were not willing to pay for me to go. Basically my father was very strict and he thought that if I went to art school I would ... he thought they were quite corrupt places, you know ... The old fashion idea of art school and what was happening so he wasn't very keen on me going and my mum thought that it was a waste of money because I would get married and have children. (Interview with Pauline Crook, 17 February 2006)

Pauline Crook was another woman artist that I interviewed for my research. Born in the post-war period, she became an artist later in life and has been exhibiting since 1981 (Figure 1). Crook's story of becoming an artist was very different and yet so close to Runayker's. Coming from a working-class background, going to an art college, was simply not an option. It was after she had worked as a secretary for many years and only after her children had gone to school that she became able to follow her dream: become a 'working artist', an interesting term she has chosen to describe herself:

> So I didn't go to art college, instead I did in fact what my mum wanted me to do, I learnt shorthand and typing and worked in offices, until I got married and had my first child which was ... 27 years ago now ... in 1979 and then I was a full-time mum for quite some years and did all sorts of odd, part-time jobs and what have you to bring a little bit more money in and then when I got to 40 and when my second daughter went off to school, I just decided I wanted to do something for myself, I wanted to ... you know, start with art up again ... I didn't ... I sort of didn't really think I would become *a working artist* and that I would have a studio at that stage, I just wanted to go back into that world, so what I did, I went to Brighton University and got myself on to what was in

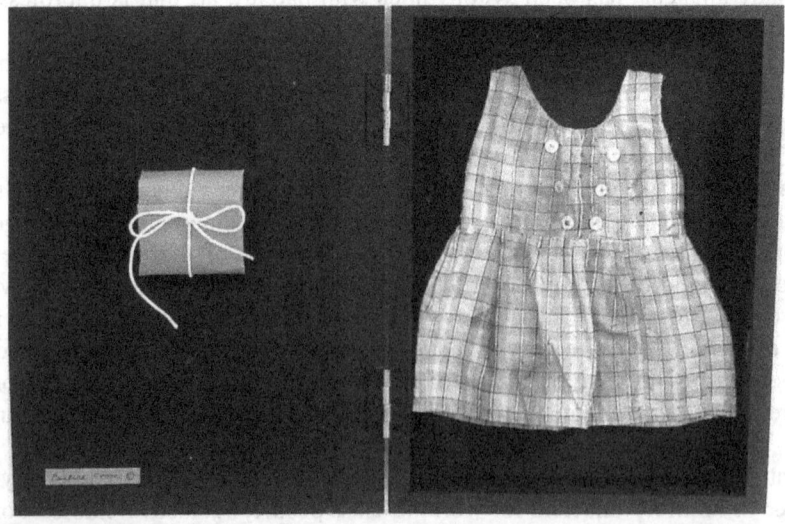

Figure 1. Pauline Crook, *My Heart is No Stone*, 3D box – mixed media (reproduced with the kind permission of the artist).

those days, called the Certificate of Art. (Interview with Pauline Crook, 17 February 2006, my emphasis)

In discussions we have held after the interview Crook has particularly emphasised and explained why she had chosen to call herself, a 'working artist': 'It took me a long time to accept that I could be taken seriously by others to be an artist (and allowed myself) – that it wasn't just a hobby but what I was (and always deep down had felt I was, even as a small child). So I guess calling myself a working artist was as much for me as anyone else!' (Crook, personal email communication). What Crook's commentary powerfully highlights here is the importance of art being recognised and registered as a legitimate kind of work and not a hobby of 'the lady artist' as also noted in Dalton's (2001) study above.

Runayker's and Crook's stories of becoming an artist further foreground the fact that women lead interrupted lives, but the schemata of these interruptions can vary: Runayker went to an art college, but had to give up practising her art to survive and support her family, while Crook had to postpone the dream of becoming an artist till her 'real duties' as a woman had been fulfilled. What is interesting in both stories however is first how these interrupted life trajectories are particularly relevant to women artists from the working classes and second how education has played a catalytic role in changing the route of their lives and opening up paths for their dreams to be sought.

In light of the complex interrelations between education and art as charted in my discussion so far, what I therefore suggest is that education and art should be analysed as an *assemblage*, a complex social entity where power relations and forces of desire are constantly at play in creating conditions of possibility for women to resist, imagine themselves becoming other and for new possibilities in their lives to be actualised. In making this proposition, I draw of course on Deleuze and Guattari's concept of *agencement* (1984, 1988) that Brian Massumi has translated as assemblage,[13] and DeLanda's redeployment of assemblage theory as 'a novel approach to social ontology' (2006, 1). I will now offer an overview of assemblage theory in relation to my specific proposition.

Glimpses into assemblage theory

As I have written elsewhere (Tamboukou 2008a), becoming an artist should be analysed as a complex social process, a machinic rather than a linear model of transformations and changes. Deleuze and Guattari's (1988) philosophical concept of the *machinic assemblage* has therefore become instrumental in such an approach; it allows for the possibility of open configurations, continuous connections and intense relations, incessantly transforming life.

Drawing on aspects of Deleuze's theorisation, Manuel DeLanda has elaborated a theory of assemblages as a new philosophical understanding of social entities that 'should account for the synthesis of the properties of a whole not reducible to its parts' (2006, 4). Conceived as a theory of 'wholes whose properties emerge from the interactions between parts' (2006, 5), the assemblage approach offered by DeLanda particularly looks into the historically difficult problem of the micro/macro relations and can therefore give 'a sense of the irreducible social complexity characterising the contemporary world' (2006, 6). Such an approach has therefore become very useful for a narrative-based analysis of the art/education encounter as an assemblage of personal stories, institutional arrangements, specific discourses and histories, and complex social and cultural networks.

As DeLanda notes, *assemblages* in Deleuze's conceptualisation are 'characterized by relations of exteriority'. This is an important aspect of the assemblage theory since *relations of exteriority* 'imply that a component part of the assemblage may be detached from it and plugged into a different assemblage in which its interactions are different' (2006, 10) As already discussed above, an assemblage as a whole is never reducible to its parts which can therefore have a variety of expressions and functions within different connections and settings. DeLanda succinctly points out that 'the exteriority of relations implies a certain autonomy for the terms they relate' (2006, 11) and consequently according to Deleuze, 'a relation may change without the terms changing' (cited in DeLanda 2006, 11). What is also crucial in Deleuze's primary configuration of the assemblage is the heterogeneity of its components. In DeLanda's reconfiguration, however, the principle of heterogeneity is not taken 'as a constant property, but as a variable that may take different values' (2006, 11).

Following Deleuze and Guattari's conceptualisation, DeLanda further charts two axes along which the concept of the assemblage can be defined. The first refers to the variety of roles that the parts of an assemblage can play, 'from a purely material role at one extreme of the axis to a purely expressive role at the other extreme', as well as 'a mixture of material and expressive roles' (2006, 12). The second axis refers to processes of territorialisation and deterritorialisation that the parts of the assemblage are constantly immersed into: the former 'stabilize the identity of an assemblage by increasing its degree of internal homogeneity' (2006, 12), while the latter destabilise the whole. Both processes can be at work simultaneously not only in different components of the assemblage but also within 'one and the same component' (2006, 12)

Let us then see how DeLanda's reconfiguration of the DeleuzoGuattarian concept of the *agencement* might be used to illuminate the art/education/social class encounter and account for the complexity of its relations and functions. To start with the first axis defined above, what can the material and expressive roles of the art/education assemblage components be about? Of course there can be a great variety of references here and the examples cannot be exclusive, but to start with components playing a material role, DeLanda notes, that 'at the very least [they] involve a set of human bodies properly oriented (physically or psychologically) towards each other' (2006, 12). Face-to-face conversations are a classic example, but also 'interpersonal networks structuring communities' and hierarchical organisations governing cities or nation-states are also used as illustrations (2006, 12). In this context, the art/education assemblage components that play a material role include amongst others, a rich network of human bodies and their interaction as well as a range of educational and art institutions in all levels of social and cultural hierarchies.

Giving examples of components that play an expressive role is rather more complicated, since in DeLanda's assemblage theory, expressivity is not reducible to language and symbols (2006, 12). Bodily expressions are sometimes as important as the content of discursive exchanges, choices made regarding the topics of discussions, as well as the network of symbolic power relations revolving around conversations and interlocutors. There is finally a matrix of social behaviours and attitudes ranging for example from expressions of solidarity in interpersonal networks to expressions of legitimacy in hierarchical organisations (DeLanda 2006, 13). It goes without saying that the art/education assemblage is rich in cases of social and cultural expressivity, particularly so I would add, when its analysis proceeds via the narrative route.

In relation to the second axis, which refers to processes of *territorialisation* and *deterritorialisation* and I would add *reterritorialisation*, things become etymologically more self-explanatory. Territorialisation and deterritorialisation both derive from the latin word *terra*, meaning earth. Both terms therefore relate to processes of grounding or uprooting. In this light, processes of *territorialisation* 'define or sharpen the spatial boundaries of actual territories' (DeLanda, 2006, 13), but they also work towards solidifying the often moving grounds of the assemblage thus 'increasing its internal homogeneity' (2006, 13). Processes of *territorialisation* are therefore always antagonistically related to processes of deterritorialisation, which 'destabilize spatial boundaries' (2006, 13) and once again create earthquakes in the grounds of the assemblage. Here again the long history of struggles for women's inclusion in the educational and cultural institutions of modernity is an excellent example of this war of discourses and processes of territorialisation and deterritorialisation.

Assemblage theory at work

Let me now give some narrative examples of the principles of the assemblage theory I have been discussing so far, drawing on the archive of women artists' auto/biographical narratives that my research has created. In this context I will first focus on a biographical extract for May Stevens (1924–), a celebrated American working-class artist[14]:

> Born in Quincy, Massachusetts, to a working-class family, May Stevens was the oldest of three children and the only girl. Her father worked as a pipefitter in the nearby shipyard, and her mother, Alice Dick Stevens, was a housewife who had dropped out of school in the eighth grade to work as a mother's helper when her own mother died. Stevens was the first member of her family to go to college. Her father approved, hoping that it would allow her to break with her working-class origins; he little suspected that it would make her 'grow her hair long, dress all in black' and ultimately end up 'identifying more with his class than he did.' Afraid that she would end up as a schoolteacher, Stevens chose the Massachusetts College of Art in Boston instead of a conventional liberal arts college. Her conviction that regardless of what else she did, she would always be an artist dates from her art school years. (Witzling 1994, 65–6)

I was intrigued by this biographical extract about the working-class artist May Stevens, which I have seen as a vivid cartography of the art/education assemblage. Not only does it boldly portray the schism between being an artist and being a schoolteacher, but it also exemplifies one of the principles of the assemblage theory I have been discussing above: the argument that 'the synthesis of the properties of the whole cannot be reducible to its parts and the consequent effect that a component part of the assemblage may be detached from it and plugged into a different assemblage in which its interactions are different' (DeLanda 2006, 10). What is then, this particular assemblage component that has had different interactions in the above example? It is, I argue, Steven's choice of the Massachusetts College of Art in Boston as a safe art college that would protect her from becoming a schoolteacher. It is indeed interesting to look back into the history of this art college for some of the assemblage theory features to be illuminated.[15]

The Massachussetts College of Art (MassArt) was founded in 1873 as the Massachusetts Normal Art School (MNAS). As an art educational institution it was a response to the growing demand for art teachers after the 1870 Industrial Drawing Act that made art education compulsory for all children in public schools in the USA.

MNAS would waive fees for students on the condition that upon their graduation, they would reside in Massachusetts and teach in public schools. It goes without saying that women comprised the majority of the body of teachers to be trained in art education and consequently of the student population of MNAS.[16] In this context, MNAS has been presented and indeed celebrated as a progressive educational institution that made art education accessible to the masses in general and women in particular: 'Massachusetts Normal Art School, revolutionised *who* could study art ... At this fledging school, art was reinterpreted as the legitimate domain of working people' (Korzenik 1987, 33).

Hand in hand with this revolution, however, went a specific vision of what art in general and art education in particular should be about when offered or made accessible to the masses. Walter Smith, the first principal of MNAS who moved from London to Boston to take up this position, was seriously involved in the aesthetics and politics of the Arts and Crafts movement; his vision was to popularise and enshrine art, a project that he was attempting to transfer from South Kensington to Boston. Art historians have indeed placed his project of promoting industrial drawing in the context of the British South Kensington System of Art Education (Stankiewicz 1992, 165). As Dalton has further pointed out: 'British art education was exported to its colonies in the late nineteenth century through systems such as the South Kensington model ... and became part of the structuring forms of art education from the United States, Canada and Australasia' (2001, 4).

MNAS was therefore initially founded as a college to train art teachers for the needs of the industrialists. However, between 1873 and 1942, which is the year when May Stevens actually enrolled in MassArt, the college had not simply changed its name; it had been deterritorialised from its initial assemblage and had been reterritorialised in a different assemblage, one that would supposedly protect a working-class woman artist from actually becoming a teacher. As already discussed, the parts of any assemblage can therefore have a variety of expressions and functions within different connections and settings. This is an effect of the relations of exteriority that characterise them and which create 'a certain autonomy for the terms they relate' to the point where 'a relation may change without the terms changing'.

What is also interesting in Steven's reconfiguration of MassArt is a discontinuity in the rift that has been historically established between Classical Art and serious educational Art Institutions and the kind of art education that was available for working-class people in general and working-class girls in particular at the turn of the nineteenth century.[17]

There are more discontinuities and ruptures to be discerned here, however, particularly in the 'relations of exteriority' that can derive from the volatile assemblage of art, art education and teaching. Judy Chicago's[18] narrative from her celebrated autobiography *Through the Flower* beautifully illustrates such relations of exteriority that have derived from the feminism/art education assemblage:

> I decided to go away from the city for a year, to look for a job at a college, some-thing that I had never done before, having supported myself by teaching occasional extension classes. *When I graduated from college I had vowed not to become involved with day school teaching*, as I didn't want to be like my teachers who had become more invested with their teaching than their art-making. Now I wanted to teach – but I wanted to teach women. I wanted to try to communicate to female students, to tell them what I had gone through in making myself into an artist. I felt that by externalizing the process I had gone through, I could examine it, which would be the first step in turning it around, and the

women's class might also be the first step in making an alternative female art community. (Chicago 1982, 67, my emphasis)

What Chicago imagines in her narrative, is an alternative female art community emerging from the previously dreaded women's art class. We know from Chicago's own experiment for a feminist art education, that this dream was actually realised, creating unforeseen results not only for the students but also for herself and for education in general:

> The class was as good for me as it was for the students. It was a wonderful experience to be able to share the struggles I had had and find that they were not only interesting and meaningful to the women, but provided them with information about how to help themselves. The one thing that I didn't understand at the time was that I had begun a process that was natural and organic. Once I had organized the class, taken it away from the school, given myself and the students a space of our own and a support group, provided them with a positive role model and an environment in which we could be ourselves, growth for all of us was inevitable. It almost didn't matter what we did as long as we were working at something productive. This suggests that what I stumbled on in Fresno has implications for all areas of female education. (Chicago 1982, 78)

Chicago's feminist art experiment deterritorialised art education from its historically imposed class and gender constraints and created conditions of possibility for relations of exteriority to be at work. What has to be reconsidered, however, in the study of events of deterritorialisation, is how classical sociological axes of difference, such as class and gender are reconfigured within the assemblage approach, as I will further discuss.

DeLanda actually suggests that social classes should be conceptualised 'as assemblages of interpersonal networks and institutional organizations' (2006, 66). Drawing on the two axes of assemblage theory as delineated above, DeLanda shows how networked communities and the institutional organisations that support and sustain them have differential access to resources and how the interplay of material and expressive roles within them mould distinctive lifestyles. In this line of analysis, the identity of a class emerges as an effect of territorialisation, which is manifested by a variety of exclusions and inclusions and is nominally coded by linguistic categories. One could ask here of course, what is so different in the assemblage approach from Bourdieu's analyses, a well-established tradition in the theorisation of social class? DeLanda actually admits that Bourdieu's theories in *Distinction* (1984) come very close to assemblage analytics: 'considering that both habits and skills, two of the components of subjectivity in assemblage theory are dispositions, most of Bourdieu's ideas would be to seem ontologically compatible with the assemblage approach' (2006, 64). Despite the analogies drawn here, there is however a big incompatibility in the two approaches according to DeLanda – the very notion of *habitus*.

Habitus of course is central in Bourdieu's theory, a master process 'that makes possible the free production of all the thoughts, perceptions and actions inherent in the particular conditions of its production and only those' (Bourdieu 1990, cited in DeLanda 2006, 65). While there is no doubt that social classes possess, manifest and reproduce their own habits, this should not necessarily mean that submission to order – a condition of possibility for the formation of habitus – is a necessary consequence. 'In the assemblage approach submission or obedience cannot be taken for granted and must always be accounted for in terms of specific enforcement mechanisms', notes DeLanda (2006, 65). Moreover whilst Bourdieu's *habitus* is mapped in an abstract social space structured by economic and cultural capital, resource distributions in assemblage theory 'are always intimately related to concrete social entities such as interpersonal networks and organizations' (DeLanda 2006, 65).

What ultimately emerges as a significant difference in the two approaches is that they rely on different theorisations of subjectivity altogether. DeLanda's is a Humean model of subjectivity, wherein experience founds the subject within 'the given' (Deleuze 1991, 104). What we can only have is 'a practical subject', not a 'knowing subject', Deleuze in his essay on Hume has succinctly remarked (1991, 120). Bourdieu's *habitus*, on the other hand, relies on 'the linguisticality of experience ... all that needs to be accounted for is the construction of subjective experience through linguistic categories' (DeLanda 2006, 66).

In light of the above, the forces that territorialise social classes are always contingent and precarious in the assemblage approach, while processes of deterritorialisation are simultaneously at work 'blurring the borders between classes [and] thus we may accept that a population of networked communities is sorted out into social classes without having to agree that these classes form a simple hierarchy' (DeLanda 2006, 67).

To return to Chicago's experiment then, spatial, institutional and class barriers territorialising art education were transgressed and the art class was reterritorialised in a safe space, one that could support and sustain women's creativity as an open process: 'it didn't matter what we did as long as we were working at something productive'. What my own research has further shown is that Chicago's experience has not been an isolated event, although the uniqueness of it should not be downplayed or surpassed as insignificant. Indeed, both Runayker's and Crook's stories discussed above, revolved around a group of women artists they were both part of and which emerged at the end of an art degree course in the UK:

> I belong to an art group, we are called *FrockArt* and there are seven of us, seven ladies, most of them I've known since the Certificate of Art, so that's going back to the beginning of the 1990s. And they are just lovely! They are my best friends, I just feel incredibly lucky. It's a very strong, solid women's group and we really care about each other and when we have our meetings – we usually meet and have lunch somewhere – we discuss all the things we have to discuss. They are such happy times and we laugh a lot. It's just lovely, a lovely, lovely group and they are all really good at what they do ... And we exhibit together, usually, well this year we haven't got too many plans because we all needed, we wanted all to experiment and see what happens, so we are hoping to exhibit at the end of the year, but last year, how many times did we exhibit? Three times last year. (Interview with Pauline Crook, 17 February 2006)

Expressions of solidarity in interpersonal networks are amongst the roles of the components of any assemblage in DeLanda's theoretical configuration; there is actually a rich mixture of material and expressive roles in Chicago's and Crook's narratives above, that deterritorialise the constraining effects of a gender-oriented art education and reterritorialise women artists within a plane of creativity and real and imagined possibilities for becoming other.

One should not become over celebratory here of course. Processes of reterritorialisation always carry the risks of creating new segmentarities and new constraints. Women's inclusion in Art Education and Art Institutions has created its own hierarchies and has generated new types of exclusion. As already noted, gender as a sociological axis of difference is again challenged in the assemblage approach, only here critical feminist theories[19] have done this well before DeLanda and sometimes in tension with Deleuze.[20] Indeed in mapping difference on three major planes, between women and men, amongst women and within each woman herself critical feminist theories have followed Scott's provocative argument that we could rewrite history, 'only if we recognize that "man" and "woman" are at once empty and overflowing categories' (1997, 167). Scott has defined 'men' and 'women' as empty categories 'because they have no ultimate, transcendent meaning' (1997, 167) and overflowing since they can never be pinned down without releasing forces of deterritorialisation. This take on gender runs in parallel with the assemblage approach; feminist theorists, however, have pointed to the necessity of keeping 'women' as a political rather than a social entity, a platform supporting women's real and multiple struggles. Assemblages after all are pragmatically as well as historically constituted entities, although the term 'historical' in DeLanda encompasses cosmological, evolutionary as well as human history (2006, 28).

Since assemblages are precarious and historically contingent entities, Deleuze and Guattari have long warned us that: 'you may make a rupture, draw a line of flight, yet there is still a danger that you will reencounter organisations that restratify everything, formations that restore power to a signifier, attributions that reconstitute a subject' (1988, 9). However in the context of Deleuze and Guattari's geophilosophy, where we start from or where we end up – beginnings and endings – are not so important. In their writings, they have actually put forward nomadic modes of existence: 'other ways of moving and traveling: proceeding from the middle, through the middle, coming and going, rather than starting and finishing' (1988, 25). What is critical in the experience of freedom is our movement in between, when we follow lines of flight or escape, the intermezzo, the process of becoming other. The importance of theorising freedom in the intermezzo brings the discussion of the paper to the central theme of this volume: thinking about resistance. As I will further argue, rethinking resistance is one of the crucial effects of engaging with the assemblage approach.

Rethinking resistance: ethics, aesthetics and politics

Drawing on insights from the assemblage approach that I have discussed so far, what I argue is that theorising resistance forces us to rethink the problem of the micro/macro relation. As a matter of fact this relation is at the heart of the way we make sense of what resistance can be about. It goes without saying that the micro/macro relation has had a long, tormented and irresolute history. As DeLanda succinctly points out: 'posing the problem correctly involves first of all, getting rid of the idea that social processes occur at only two levels, the micro- and the macro-levels, particularly when these levels are conceived in terms of reified generalities like "the individual" and society as a whole' (2006, 32). There is indeed a body of sociological theory that has addressed this problem.[21] What is critical in the assemblage approach however is that individuals themselves are taken as assemblages of sub-personal components: 'the subject emerges as relations of exteriority are established between the contents of experience' (2006, 47). What we therefore have in unravelling the micro/macro relation is a complex encounter of flux subjectivities always in the process of becoming within multiscaled social realities both spatially and temporally. If we remember that these multiscaled social realities can never be reducible to their components, it derives that they can causally affect their components in both limiting and enabling ways, but also that their interactions cannot be simply attributed to their components. In this context, the subjects emerging in the assemblage approach can act in a variety of ways that do not necessarily or automatically involve submission or resistance. Such events or schemata and models of social interaction should always be accounted for, in terms of context-specific analyses and it is in the specific context of the social milieu of art that I will now focus.

As I have pointed out in the beginning of this paper, the Foucauldian idea of making one's life a work of art has been central in the overall project of writing a genealogy of women artists. Indeed drawing on my previous research with women teachers' narratives, I have argued that women artists' practices mapped within the art/education assemblage have opened up smooth spaces for an aesthetics of existence. This is a political project *par excellence*, intervening in and interrupting 'the distribution of the sensible', a conceptual configuration that Jacques Rancière has offered as a ground wherein aesthetic and political practices meet: 'I call the distribution of the sensible the system of self-evident facts of sense perception that simultaneously discloses the existence of something in common and the delimitations that define the respective parts and positions within it' (2009, 12). The 'distribution of the sensible' is therefore a system where inclusion and exclusion work hand by hand in defining the grounds, subjects and implicit laws of certain communities of practice and thought.[22] As Rancière suggests, 'the distribution of the sensible reveals who can have a share in what is common to the community based on what they do and on the time and space in which this activity is performed' (2009, 12). This is the point where he rigorously argues that 'there is "an aesthetics" at the core of politics', linking here his understanding of aesthetics and politics to Foucault's ethics and aesthetics of the self (2009, 13).

Women artists' practices as inscribed in their narratives create a powerful exemplar for Rancière's analysis and particularly for the way he links aesthetics and politics in the 'distribution of the sensible'. His particular reference to 'the properties of spaces and possibilities of times' (2009, 13) in delimiting who could be included in the community of artists, has been particularly fleshed out in the rich themes that have emerged from women artists' narratives. Having intervened in the aesthetics of the distribution of the sensible, women artists' practices have thus sided with what Rancière (2009, 29–30) has identified as the crucial link between 'the "aesthetic" avant-garde and the "political" avant-garde: the invention of sensible forms and material structures for a life to come', a kind of 'aesthetic anticipation of the future'.

Art as critique is therefore extended to art as a way of life – art and life becoming constitutive of each other, as in Foucault's provocative statement that we should make our life a work of art (1986, 351) In fleshing out this suggestion, Jon Simons (1995, 76) has discerned three central themes in the Foucauldian aesthetics of the self: demands of style, artistic practice as a source of empowerment, and working with present conditions and limits. In Simon's analysis, *the demands of style* is the never-ending struggle for transgressing the limits that constrain but at the same time define the very existence of human beings. Artistic practices create possibilities for transgression and thus become a source of empowerment and sites for the emergence of new subjectivities: 'one creates new modalities of subjectivity in the same way that an artist creates new forms from the palette' (Guattari 1995, 7).

The artist's hand and mind are thus crucial for the creation of new forms, in life and in art. Since an artist knows that 'creation of form is not a matter of spontaneity, impulsiveness, licentious abandonment and irresponsible energy' (Simons 1995, 77), she can more easily transfer the artistic experience and practice in creating new forms for her life, 'new modalities of subjectivity'. Moreover artists know that artistic practices work better when there is a need, an urgency, a question to be answered, a problem to be resolved. Foucault has drawn on this agonistic character of the artistic practice in its transposition as a practice on the self.[23]

What is crucial in considering women artists' technologies of the self is that the artistic practice and the self technology often converge: 'I am never so happy as when I paint' has become a *refrain* of the women artist's auto/biographical narratives I have analysed and in this sense I argue, women artists paint so as to become other. And yet this creation, these becomings have to be actualised within present conditions and limits: 'depending on the balance between enabling limits and constraining limitations, between lightness and heaviness, we have more or less capacity to create ourselves as works of art', notes Simons. This last theme of 'working within present conditions and limits' in the Foucauldian aesthetics of the self makes connections with the Humean model of subjectivity within assemblage theory, Deleuze's assertion as I have already noted that 'subjectivity is essentially *practical* [and] the subject is constituted within the given' (1991, 104).

In this context assemblage theory throws light into women artists' complex interrelation with their social milieus in the process of resisting what they are, by continuously becoming other. These becomings are not always conscious or necessarily agentic, but they are not totally contingent either. Becoming is I argue another way of thinking about resistance when you have stepped outside a juridical model of power, 'that which lays down the law, which prohibits, which refuses and which has a whole range of negative effects: exclusion, rejection, denial, obstruction, occultation' (Foucault 1980a, 183).

In the same configuration that resistance is immanent in *dispositifs* of non-juridical models of *power*, 'there are no relations of power without resistances' Foucault (1980b, 142) has famously asserted, *lines of flight* and *becomings* are immanent in *agencements*. As already noted, assemblages are being constituted through processes of territorialisation and deterritorialisation. This is, however, where we have to work to respond to a crucial problem that Deleuze has raised in relation to resistance:

> On the side of lines of resistance or what I call lines of flight: How should we conceive of the relations or conjugations, the processes of unification? I would say that the collective field of immanence in which *agencements* are made at a given moment, and where they trace their lines of flight, also have a veritable diagram. It is necessary then to find the complex *agencement* capable of actualizing this diagram, by bringing about the conjunction of lines or points of deterritorialization. (Deleuze 1997, 191)

Deleuze points to the necessity of charting cartographies of lines of flight; these diagrams will function as continually destabilising and challenging, what we think and what we do, 'the distribution of the sensible' as discussed above, but how can this be done? Creating archives of narratives of resistance is, I suggest, a way of responding to the problem raised by Deleuze and this is how I return to narratives by way of concluding this paper.

Narratives of becoming as cartographies of resistance

Both Foucault and Deleuze were preoccupied with the notion of becoming in the context of rethinking time in philosophy. Foucault's genealogical problem actually starts from a problematisation of the historicity of our present, and the possibilities of opening it up to radical futures. Deleuze's work has been particularly attentive to the latter: planes of open futurity. As Rajchman (2009, 47) has poetically put it, for Foucault, a history of the present 'is a history of the portion of the past that we don't see is still with us', while for Deleuze the diagnosis of the past was not as important as the imagination of the untimely future, 'to be attentive to the unknown that is knocking at the door' (cited in ibid.). Becoming is then always a process that is set into motion by the will to lose the self, leave the grounds on which you think you stand on, follow lines of flight, deterritorialise and disperse the self. Becoming is thus an open process, a nomadic journey, a wandering:

> Becoming is a rhizome, not a classificatory or genealogical tree. Becoming is certainly not imitating, or identifying with something; neither is it regressing-progressing; neither is it corresponding, establishing corresponding relations; neither is it producing, producing a filiation or producing through filiation. Becoming is a verb with a consistency all its own; it does not reduce to, or lead back to, 'appearing,' 'being,' 'equaling,' or 'producing'. (Deleuze and Guattari 1988, 239)

As I have shown in the discussion of this paper, women artists' narratives trace lines of flight and recount events of becoming other. But as I have also pointed out, leaving the self always entails the risk of reterritorialisation within new segmentarities: 'What is it which tells us that, on a line of flight, we will not rediscover everything we were fleeing?' (Deleuze and Parnet 2002, 38). However, the end is never important when you trace a line of flight, what is always more interesting and fascinating is the experience of being in the middle, the intermezzo, the strength to take up fragments and loose ends of broken lines of flight. This is, according to Deleuze, another way of beginning, another way of becoming: 'to take up the interrupted line, to join a segment to the broken line, to make it pass between two rocks in a narrow gorge, or over the top of the void, where it had stopped' (ibid., 39). These new beginnings in the middle always appear as discontinuous and fragmented events that can only leave their traces in narratives. As Deleuze has argued, the event is always elusive and cannot be reached: 'The pure event is tale and novella, never an actuality' (Deleuze 2001, 73). Women artists' narratives were indeed rich in recounting 'new beginnings in the middle', 'interrupted lines taken up again', 'passages between rocks'. Runayker's narrative of how her canvases were filled with images of the harsh life that had intervened in and interrupted her career as an artist has become an exemplar of the possibilities opened up by taking up broken lines. As she has vigorously asserted, her story has destabilised the myth of continuity as a *sine qua non* condition of an artist's career. Runayker's and Crook's narratives have indeed fleshed out the experience of new beginnings in the middle as another way of becoming.[24] What I therefore suggest is that brought together on a plane of what Deleuze has identified as 'minor knowledges' (1997, 192), women artists' narratives create archives of radical futurity: they offer possibilities both for their narrators and readers/narratees 'of becoming untimely, of placing ourselves outside the constraints, the limitations and blinkers of the present' (Grosz 2004, 117), of imagining a future, a world, a people yet to come.

Notes
1. The artists Irene Runayker and Pauline Crook, whose narratives I draw on in this paper, have asked me to use their real name.
2. Runayker's paintings are available at: http://www.irenerunayker.com.
3. AHRC award: B/SG/AN10693/APN17267, 2004–2005.
4. See Tamboukou (2010).

5. See Tamboukou (2008b) for an extensive discussion of a genealogical approach to narratives.
6. See Tamboukou (2008a).
7. For an overview, see Squire, Andrews, and Tamboukou (2008) and Riessmann-Kohler (2008).
8. See Tamboukou (2003).
9. In arguing that Foucault's *technologies of the self* need to be gendered I have traced genealogical lines in the care of the female self and have shown how women teachers have decisively bent the lines traced by Foucault. See Tamboukou (2003).
10. Maynard's unpublished autobiography, chap. 35, 386, Queen Mary and Westfield College Archives.
11. Maynard's, unpublished autobiography, chap. 44, 2–3.
12. See, amongst others, Cherry (1993).
13. The notion of *agencement* has been translated as assemblage by Brian Massumi (Deleuze and Guattari 1988), however some commentators have suggested that the term does not have a suitable English equivalent. As translator Daniel W. Smith explains, *agencement* comes from the verb *agencer* which means 'to put together, organize, order, lay out, arrange' (Deleuze 1997, 183); these notions are probably more complicated than just assemble.
14. For an overview of the artist's work, see http://www.artcyclopedia.com/artists/stevens_may.html
15. See Tamboukou (2010).
16. Massachusetts College of Arts, Archive, 1998, 3.
17. See Tamboukou (2010) for a detailed discussion of the cultural hierarchies in Boston and the rift between the School of the Museum of the Fine Arts and the Massachusetts Normal Art School.
18. Chicago's work can be seen on her website (http://www.judychicago.com/).
19. Critical feminisms are those feminist positions that according to Braidotti (1991) have attempted to express the female self as incomplete, plural, fragmented and yet rooted in her bodily reality. (See Tamboukou (2003) for an overview and critical discussion of this literature in relation to 'technologies of the female self'.)
20. See Buchanan and Colebrook (2000) for encounters and tensions between Deleuze and feminist theories.
21. For an overview of this literature, see DeLanda (2006, 127–8).
22. The 'sensible' here should not be understood as something that makes sense, but as something that can be perceived by the senses, 'what is visible and audible as well as what can be said, thought, made or done' (Rancière 2009, 85).
23. As I have discussed elsewhere in detail, *askesis* is central in Foucault's theorisation of *the technologies of the self* and in women's reconfiguration of them in their auto/biographical narratives. See Tamboukou (2003).
24. Throughout my genealogical project in the constitution of the female self in art I have traced a series of intermezzo becomings. See Tamboukou (2010).

References

Bourdieu, P. 1984. *Distinction: A social critique of the judgement of taste.* Trans. R. Nice. London: Routledge and Kegan Paul. (Orig. pub. 1979.)
Bourdieu, P. 1990. *The logic of practice.* Trans. R. Nice. Cambridge: Polity Press.
Braidotti, R. 1991. *Patterns of dissonance.* Cambridge: Polity Press.
Buchanan, I., and C. Colebrook, eds. 2000. *Deleuze and feminist theory.* Edinburgh: Edinburgh University Press.
Cherry, D. 1993. *Painting women: Victorian women artists.* London: Routledge.
Chicago, J. 1982. *Through the flower.* London: The Women's Press.
Copelman, D. 1985. Women in the classroom struggle: elementary school teachers in London (1870–1914). PhD thesis, Princeton University.
Copelman, D. 1996. *London's women teachers: Gender, class, and feminism, 1870–1930.* London: Routledge.
Dalton, P. 2001. *The gendering of art education: Modernism, identity and critical feminism.* Buckingham, UK: Open University Press.

DeLanda, M. 2006. *A new philosophy of society: Assemblage theory and social complexity.* London: Continuum.
Deleuze, G. and F. Guattari. 1984. *Anti-Oedipus: capitalism and schizophrenia.* Trans. R. Hurley, M. Seem and H.R. Lane. London: The Athlone Press (Orig. pub. 1972).
Deleuze, G. 1991. *Empiricism and subjectivity: An essay on Hume's Theory of Human Nature.* Trans. C.V. Boundas. New York: Columbia University Press.
Deleuze, G. 1997. Desire and pleasure. In *Foucault and his interlocutors,* ed. A.I. Davidson, 183–92. Trans. D.W. Smith. Chicago: The University of Chicago Press.
Deleuze, G. 2001. *The logic of sense.* Trans. M. Lester. London: Continuum (orig. pub. 1969).
Deleuze, G., and F. Guattari. 1988. *A thousand plateaus: Capitalism and schizophrenia.* Trans. B. Massumi. London: The Athlone Press. (Orig. pub. 1980.)
Deleuze, G. and Parnet, C. 2002. *Dialogues II.* Trans. H. Tomlinson and B. Habberjam. London: Continuum (orig. pub. 1977).
Foucault, M. 1980a. 'The history of sexuality', an interview. In *Power/knowledge: Selected interviews and other writings 1972–1977,* ed. C. Gordon, 83–193. Trans. C. Gordon. London: Harvester Wheatsheaf.
Foucault, M. 1980b. 'Powers and strategies', an interview. In *Power/knowledge: Selected interviews and other writings 1972–1977,* ed. C. Gordon, 134–45. Trans. C. Gordon. London: Harvester Wheatsheaf.
Foucault, M. 1986. On the genealogy of ethics: An overview of work in progress. In *The Foucault Reader,* ed. P. Rabinow, 340–72. Harmondsworth: Peregrine.
Foucault, M. 1988. Technologies of the self. In *Technologies of the self,* ed. L.H. Martin, H. Gutman, and P.H. Hutton, 16–49. London: Tavistock,.
Grosz, E. 2004. *The nick of time: Politics, evolution and the untimely.* Durham, NC: Duke University Press.
Guattari, F. 1995. *Chaosmosis: an ethico-aesthetic paradigm.* Trans. P. Bains and J. Pefanis. Sydney: Power Publications (Orig. pub. 1992).
Korzenik, D. 1987. The art education of working women, 1873–1903. In *From pilgrims and pioneers: New England women in the art,* ed. A. Faxon and S. Moore, 33–42. New York: Midmarch Arts Press.
Rajchman, J. 2009. Diagram and diagnosis. In *Becomings: Explorations in time, memory and futures,* ed. E. Grosz, 42–54. Ithaca, NY: Cornell University Press.
Rancière, J. 2009. *The politics of aesthetics.* Trans. G. Rochill. London: Continuum.
Riessman-Kohler, C. 2008. *Narrative methods for the human sciences.* London: Sage.
Scott, J.W. 1997. Gender: A useful category of historical analysis. In *Feminism and history,* ed. J. Scott, 152–80. Oxford: Oxford University Press.
Simons, J. 1995. *Foucault and Political.* London: Routledge.
Smith, M. 1892. *Schoolmistress and nonconformist, autobiography.* London and Carlisle: Benrose and Sons.
Squire, C., Andrews, M., and Tamboukou, M. 2008. What is narrative research? In *Doing narrative research,* ed. M. Andrews, C. Squire, and M. Tamboukou, 1–21. London: Sage.
Stankiewicz, M.A. 1992. From the Aesthetic Movement to the Arts and Crafts Movement. *Studies in Art Education* 33: 165–73.
Tamboukou, M. 2003. *Women, education, the Self: a Foucauldian perspective.* Basingstoke: Palgrave Macmillan.
Tamboukou, M. 2008a. Machinic assemblages: Women, art education and space. *Discourse: Studies in the Cultural Politics of Education* 29, no. 3: 359–75.
Tamboukou, M. 2008b. A Foucauldian approach to narratives. In *Doing narrative research,* ed. M. Andrews, C. Squire and M. Tamboukou, 102–20. London: Sage.
Tamboukou, M. 2010. *In the fold between power and desire, women artists narratives.* Newcastle-upon-Tyne: Cambridge Scholars Publishing.
Witzling, M.R., ed. 1994. *Voicing today's visions: Writings by contemporary women artists.* New York: Universe Publishing.

Index

Page numbers in **Bold** represent figures.

Abram, J. 47
activism 19, 41; feminist 27–36
African Charter on the Rights and Welfare of the Child (ACRWC) 28
African feminist theory 3–4, 23–38; Botswana education policy 27–9; children's voices 29–31; gender and education research methods 23–36; gender order and triple oppression 31–3; gender violence and *durbar* 29–31; healing methods promotion 34–6; voices of resistance and use of song 34–6
African National Congress (ANC) 16–17
Agamben, G. 80
agencement 91–101
aggression 40–50
AIDS and HIV transmission 12–13, 32
Aikman, S. 16
Alexander, E.: *et al* 29
Ali, S. 2–5, 53–67
Althusser, L. 1
Ankersmitt, F. 81
Arakmbut people (Amazonian Peru) 16
Araya Gomez, G. 70
Ardévol, E. 70
Arnot, M. 11; David, M. and Weiner, G. 15; and Fennell, S. 2, 23–4, 35
art education 85–102; assemblage theory 91–7; cartographies of resistance 99–100; ethics, aesthetics and politics 97–9; women's narratives 85–100
Arts and Crafts movement 94
Arts and Humanities Research Council (AHRC) 87; Genealogy of Women Artists project 87
Ashcroft, B.: Griffiths, G. and Tiffin, H. 24
assemblage theory 6, 85–100; and women artists 91–7
Australia 18–19

Bakare-Yusuf, B. 14
Bantu people (South Africa) 25
being-for-self-and-others 25
Bell, D. 12
Bell, V. 73
bio-politics 1–2
Bion, W. 41
Black British feminism 4–5, 53–67; audience questions 62–7; intersectionality 53–67; resistance in education 53–67; roundtable discussion 53–67; systems and subjectivities 58 *Black British Feminism* (Ali, *et al*) 66
Blackburn, J. 19
Botswana, gender and education research 23–38; liberal feminism and equality policies 27–9; Primary and Junior Secondary schools 29–31
Botswana University 3, 23–38
Bourdieu, Pierre 95; *Distinction* 95; *habitus* 95–6
Brighton University 90
British Psychoanalytical Society 42; Controversial Discussions between Melanie Klein and Anna Freud 42
British South Kensington System of Art Education 94
Britzman, D. 2–5, 39–52, 69–71; gender lecturing, a psychoanalytical discussion 39–51
Brontë, Anne 89; *Tenant of Wildfell Hall* 89
Buenos Aires 69–83; extreme urban poverty 69–82; the *zanjon* 76–80, **77–8**
Bulbeck, C. 14; *Re-orienting Western Feminisms* 14
Bunwaree, S.: and Heward, C. 11, 17
Butler, J. 1, 5, 42, 63, 73–4

Camberwell School of Arts and Crafts 85
Central School of Art 85
Centre for Rights, Equalities and Social Justice 4
Chambers, R. 27
Chicago, J. 94–6; *Through the Flower* 94–5
Children in Need of Care Regulations (2005) 29
Children's Act (1981) 29
Chilisa, B. 2–4; and Ntseane, G. 3–4, 23–38

INDEX

Clinton, Hilary 60
collectivisation 58
Collins, P. 25–6, 36, 53, 66
colonialism 14–19
Connell, R. 2–4, 9–21; Kartini's children 3, 9–19
Convention on the Rights of the Child (CRC) 28
Coordinación Ecológica Area Metropolitana Sociedad Del Estado (CEAMSE) 79–82
Copelman, D. 88
Corke, H. 88; *Neutral Ground* 88
Crenshaw, K. 53, 56–63; and Ensler, E. 59–60
Crook, P. 90–1, **90**, 96, 100
curriculum 18–19

Dalton, P. 89–91, 94
David, M.: Weiner, G. and Arnot, M. 15
Davidson, K.: and Frank, B. 15
Davies, A. 60
Davies, M. 75
De Certeau, M. 71
decolonising theory and methodologies 14
deconstructionist gender theory 3, 9–19
DeLanda, M. 91–100
Deleuze, G.: and Guattari, F. 5–6, 69–82, 87, 91–100
Descartes, René 25
Deserted Wife's and Children's Protection 29
destruction and creativity 47–8
deterritorialisation 93–100
Dillard, C. 25–6
dispositifs of power 85–100
dividing practices 2
Domingues, J. 16
Donner, H. 16
Dube, M. 26
Dunne, M.: *et al* 31–2

East London University 6, 85–102
education: resistance in 53–67; schooling and desiring 69–83
Elabor-Idemudia, P. 27
Elimination of All Forms of Discrimination Against Women Convention 19, 28
Emotional Life of Civilised Men and Women (Klein and Riviere) 40
epistemophilia 40
Escolas Normais 16
essentialisation 60–1
European Journal of Women's Studies 58
existence in relation 25
extraversion 14
extreme urban poverty 5–6, 69–83; everyday banality 74–80; the neighbourhood 70–2; schooling and desiring 69–82; workshop and video 70–82

femininity and masculinity: fantasies 4, 39–51
feminism 13–19; and art education 85–102; India 13; liberal 27–9; romancing the state 17; South Africa 13–14; theory of citizenship 13
Feminist Review 61
Fennell, S.: and Arnot, M. 2, 23–4, 35
Foley, D. 18
Fortune (magazine) 13
Foucault, Michel 1–2, 5–6, 72, 87, 98–100
Frank, B.: and Davidson, K. 15
Freud, Sigmund 1
FrockArt 96
frustration and confusion 49–50

Gender and Development (GAD) policy 28
Gender and Education Association (GEA) Conference 1–2, 53–67; Butler and Beyond 1; Regulation and Resistance 1–6
Gender and Education forum 11
gender equality in education index (GEEI) 28
gender equality in education world-wide 9–21; categorical policy and local research 10–11; colonisation and globalisation 11–13; interplay 14–17; justice arena researchers 18–19; policy issues 17–18; theorisation 13–14
Gender Equity Taskforce 11
gender lecturing 39–52; affect 43–6; clinical knowledge 46–7; clinical material 47–50; madness 39–43, 50–1; paranoid schizoid position 44–6
gender theory: deconstructionist 3, 9–19
gender transformations 3, 13–14
gender trouble 42
Gillborn, D.: and Youdell, D. 16
Gilroy, P. 67
Girton College 88
global metropole 13–19
Goduka, I. 25
Gott, J. 61
Green, A. 45–7
Griffiths, G.: Tiffin, H. and Ashcroft, B. 24
Grinberg, S. 2, 5–6, 69–83
Grosz, E. 100
Guattari, F.: and Deleuze, G. 5–6, 69–82, 87, 91–100

habitus 95–6
Hall, S. 55, 58
Hamilton, C. 88
Harding, S. 26
heterosexual matrix 1
Heward, C.: and Bunwaree, S. 11, 17
HIV and AIDS transmission 12–13, 32
Holloway, W. 65
Hountondji, P. 14

Hudson-Weems, C. 25
Hughes, M. 88
Human Rights: Universal Declaration 19
Hume, David 96

immigration issues 2
Industrial Drawing Act (1870) 93–4
Inner London Education Authority 85
Institute of Education (IOE) 1–5
intersectional feminist approaches 5, 53–67, see also Black British feminism

Jayawardena, C. 12
Johnson, P. 13
Johnson-Bailey, J. 25, 36
Jónasdóttir, A. 13

Kartini, Raden Ayu 3, 9–19; letters to Stella Zeehandelaar 9–10
Keraetse court case (1995) 29
Kgathileng court case (1993) 29
Klein, M. 4; and Riviere, J. 39–51
Kolkata research 16–17
Korzenik, D. 94
Kristeva, J. 81

Leach, F. 30–1; and Mitchell, C. 30
Livingstone, Grace 2, 55–6, 64
London Institute of Psychoanalysis 40
London School of Economics 4
Lord, A. 66; *Sister Outsider* 66
Love, Hate and Reparation (Klein and Riviere) 40–6

McDougall, J. 47; *Donald Winnicott the Man* 47
McNay, L. 72
maiming 49–50
Malaysia 17
Mama, A. 61
Maoris of New Zealand 14–15
Marshall, C.: and Young, M. 26, 29–31, 35
masculinity and femininity: fantasies 4, 39–51
Massachusetts College of Art (MassArt, Boston) 93–4
Massachusetts Normal Art School (MNAS) 93–4
Massumi, B. 91, 101
Maynard, C. 88
Mekgwe, P. 24
menstruation: first (*go rupa*) 29–32
Mies, M. 12; *Patriarchy and Accumulation on a World Scale* 14
Millennium Development Goals (MDG) 9–10
Miller, P. 15

Mirza, H. 2–5, 53–67; *Young Female and Black* 62
Mitchell, C.: and Leach, F. 30
Mitchell, J. 46
modernising offensive 16–17
Mohanty, C.T. 3, 14, 24
Moodie, T.: and Ndatshe, V. 12
Morrell, R. 16–17
Mudimbe, V. 15

Närhinen, A.: Siukola, R. and Varanka, J. 18
Ndatshe, V.: and Moodie, T. 12
neo-liberalism 16–17, 71–2
Nietzsche, Friedrich 74
Nnameka, O. 35–6
Not in my Name (Crenshaw and Ensler) 59–60
Ntseane, G.: and Chilisa, B. 3–4, 23–38
Ntseane, P. 34
Nymark, E.: and Saavedra, C. 26

Obama, Barrack 59–60, 64
O'Malley, P. 72; Valverde, M. and Rose, N. 72
Organisation for Economic Co-operation and Development (OECD) 16
othering ideologies 24, 31, 43; motherhood 24–5
Oyéwùmi, O. 14, 25

Peterson, V. 12
Phoenix, A. 2–5, 53–67
Pink, S. 70
Pitt, A. 42
Plato 32
Pong, S. 17
Poplars Dramatic Society 88
poststructural feminism 1
poverty *see* extreme urban poverty
Prins, B. 58
projective identification 46–7
Puget Sound University (Seattle) 2
Purkayastha, B.: *et al* 13
Puwar, N. 61

queer theory and politics 1, 13–14

Race Ethnicity and Education (journal) 54
racial marginalisation 2
Rajchman, J. 100
Rancière, J. 98
Reed, Yaa Asantewaa 25
Renold, E.: and Ringrose, J. 1
Rickman, J. 45, 50
Rights of the Child Declaration 19
Ringrose, J. 5, 53–67, 81; and Renold, E. 1
Riviere, J. 4; and Klein, M. 39–51

INDEX

Robinson, K. 9
Rose, J. 41–2; *Why war?* 42
Rose, N.: O'Malley, P. and Valverde, M. 72
Runayker, Irene 85–101

Saavedra, C.: and Nymark, E. 26
Sandoval, C. 26
Scarfone, D. 47
Schofield, T. 10
schooling and desiring: extreme urban poverty 69–83
Scott, J. 97
separateness 44, 48–50
sex tourism 12–13
Shakespeare, William: *Hamlet* 48
Simons, J. 98–9
Siukola, R.: Varanka, J. and Närhinen, A. 18
Slade School of Fine Art (London) 88
Smith, L. 14
Smith, M. 87
Smith, W. 94
South Bank University 55, 61
space invaders 61
Spivak, G. 24, 59
Stankiewicz, M. 94
Stauffer, R. 12
Stevens, M. 6, 93–4
Stromquist, N. 17–18
subjectivity 1
Sydney University 3, 9–21

Tamboukou, M. 6, 85–102
territorialisation 93–100
reterritorialisation 93–100
Thayer-Bacon, B. 32
Thomas Coram Research Unit 4–5
Tiffin, H.: Ashcroft, B. and Griffiths, G. 24
transnationalism 67
Tswana people and culture 23–36; story of origin 33

United Nations 11; Division for the Advancement of Women 11, 18
United Nations Children's Fund (UNICEF) 30; *Telling Their Stories* 30
United Nations Educational, Scientific and Cultural Organisation (UNESCO): Education for All 10; *Gender and Education for All* report 10
Universal Declaration of Human Rights 19
Universidad Nacional de San Martin (Buenos Aires) 5, 69–83
Unterhalter, E. 10–11, 26–7

Valdés, T. 14, 18
Valverde, M.: Rose, N. and O'Malley, P. 72
Varanka, J.: Närhinen, A. and Siukola, R. 18
Victorian Certificate of Education (VCE) 19
visibility 61

Weiner, G.: Arnot, M. and David, M. 15
Westfield College 88
Williams, W. 12
Willis, P. 62; *Learning to Labour* 62, 81
Winnicott, D. 4, 39–51; and creativity 47–50
Witzling, M. 93
womanism 25
Women of African and Asian Descent 56, 66–7
Women in Development (WID) movement 17–18, 27–9
women's labour 12
World Bank 16–17

York University (Toronto) 39–52
Yoruba society (West Africa) 14
Youdell, D. 81; and Gillborn, D. 16
Young, M.: and Marshall, C. 26, 29–31, 35